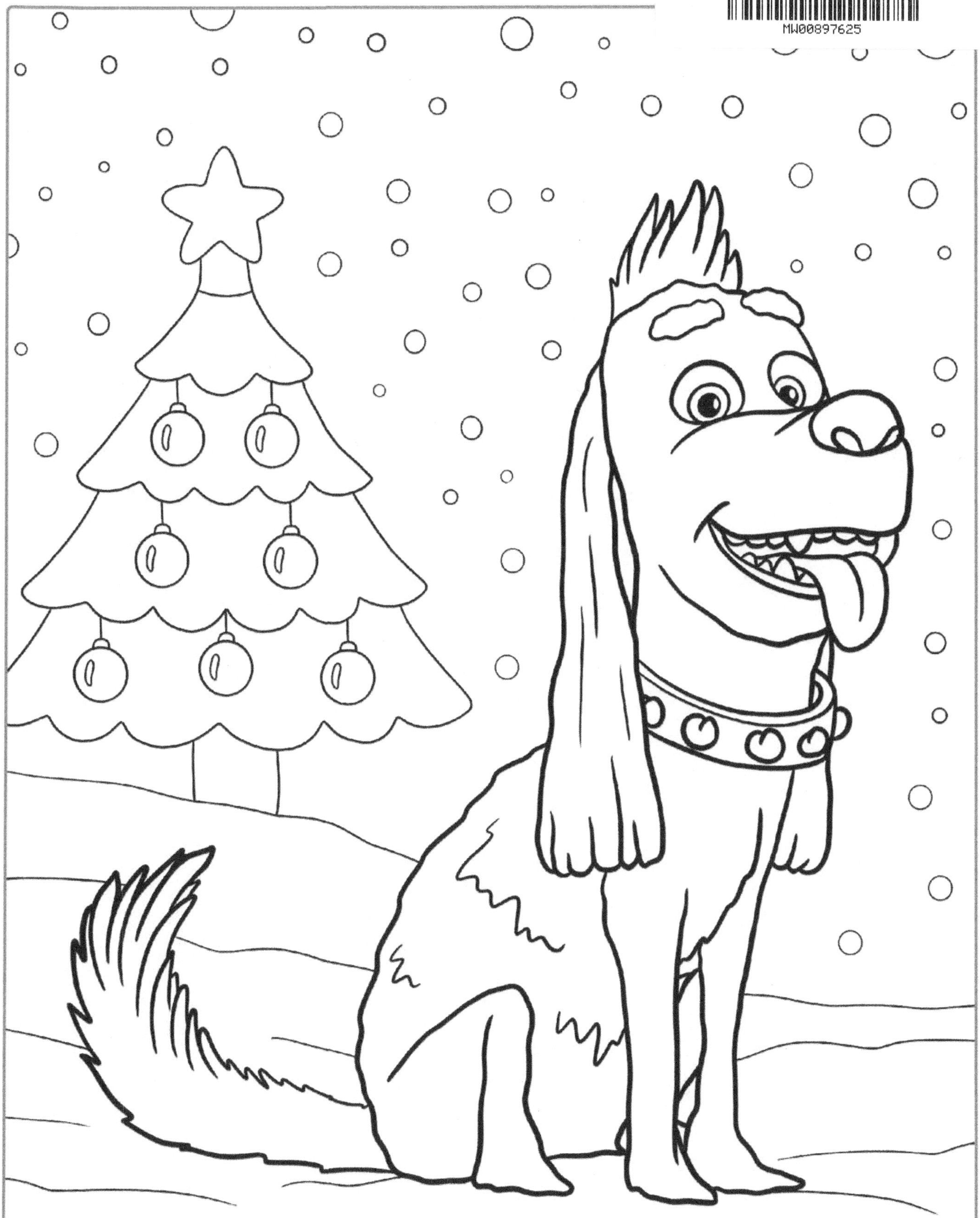

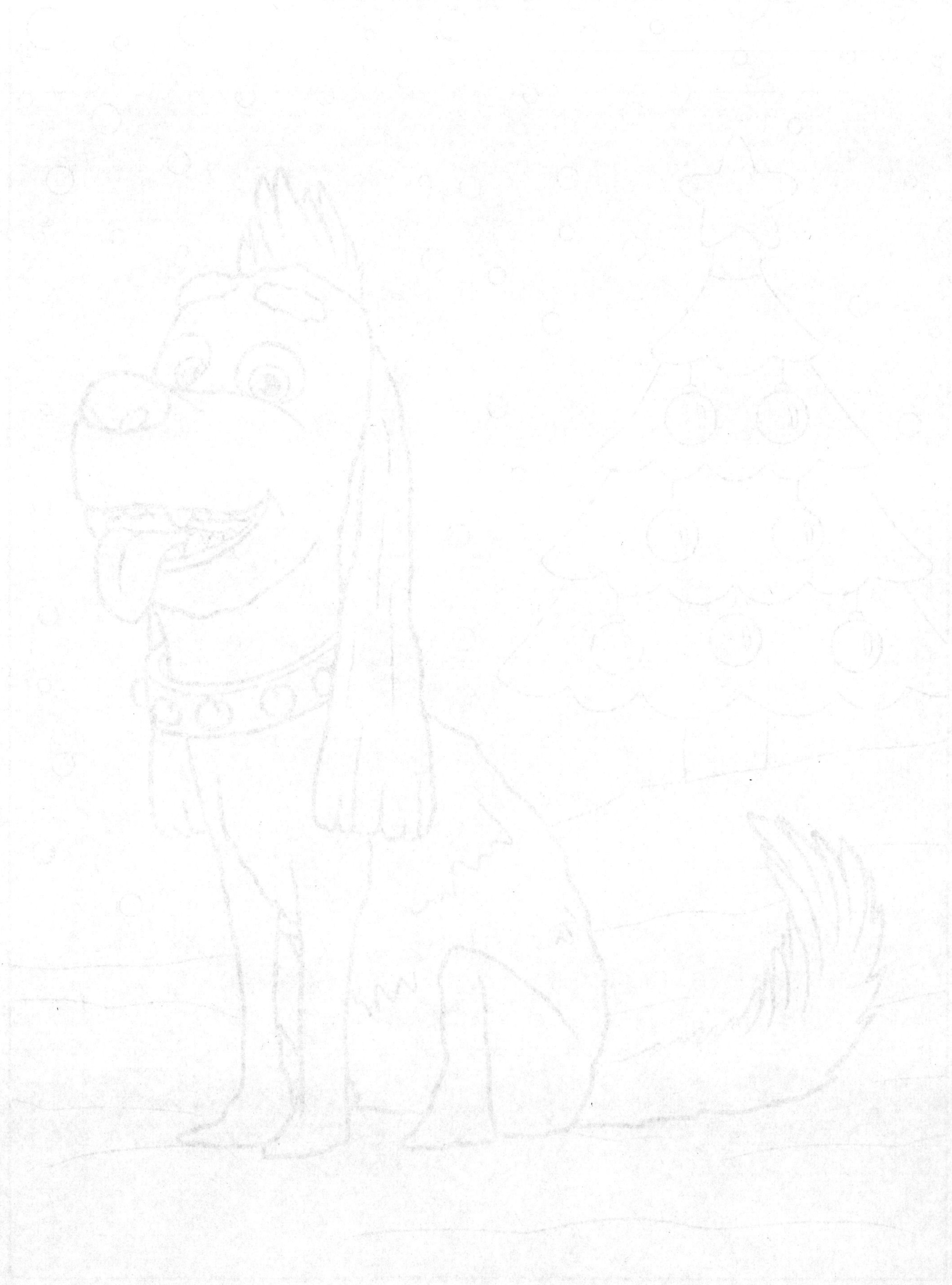

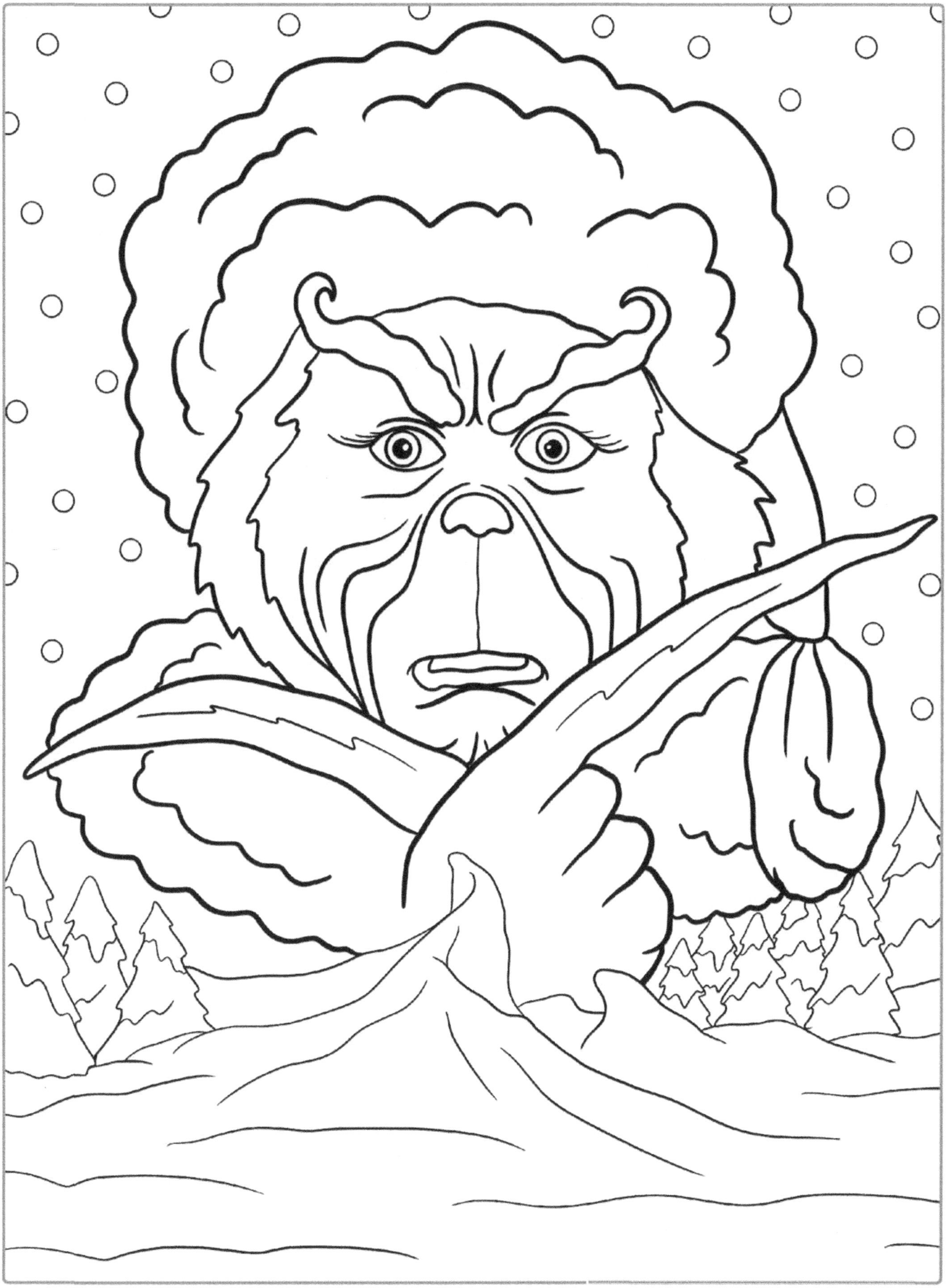

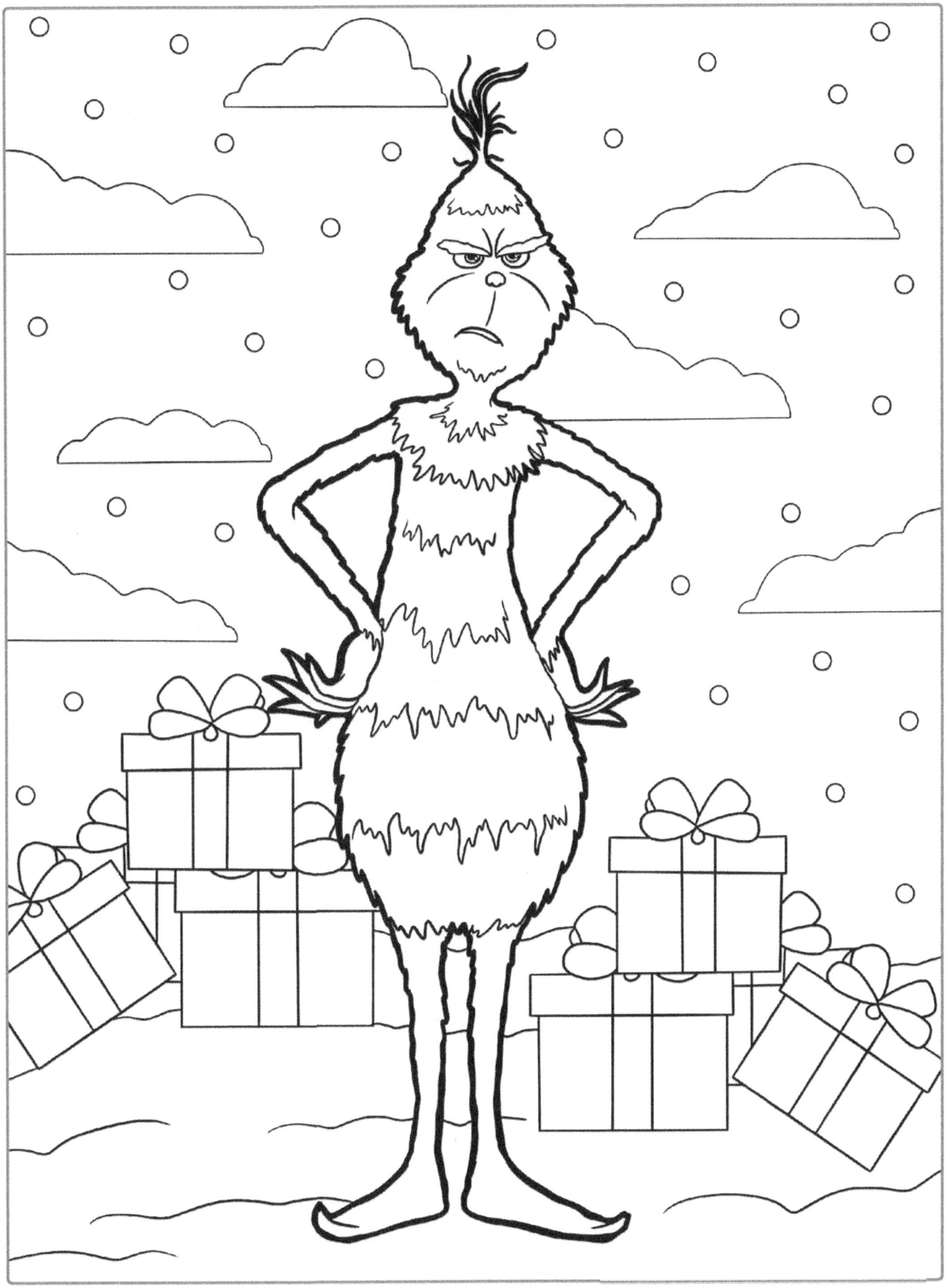

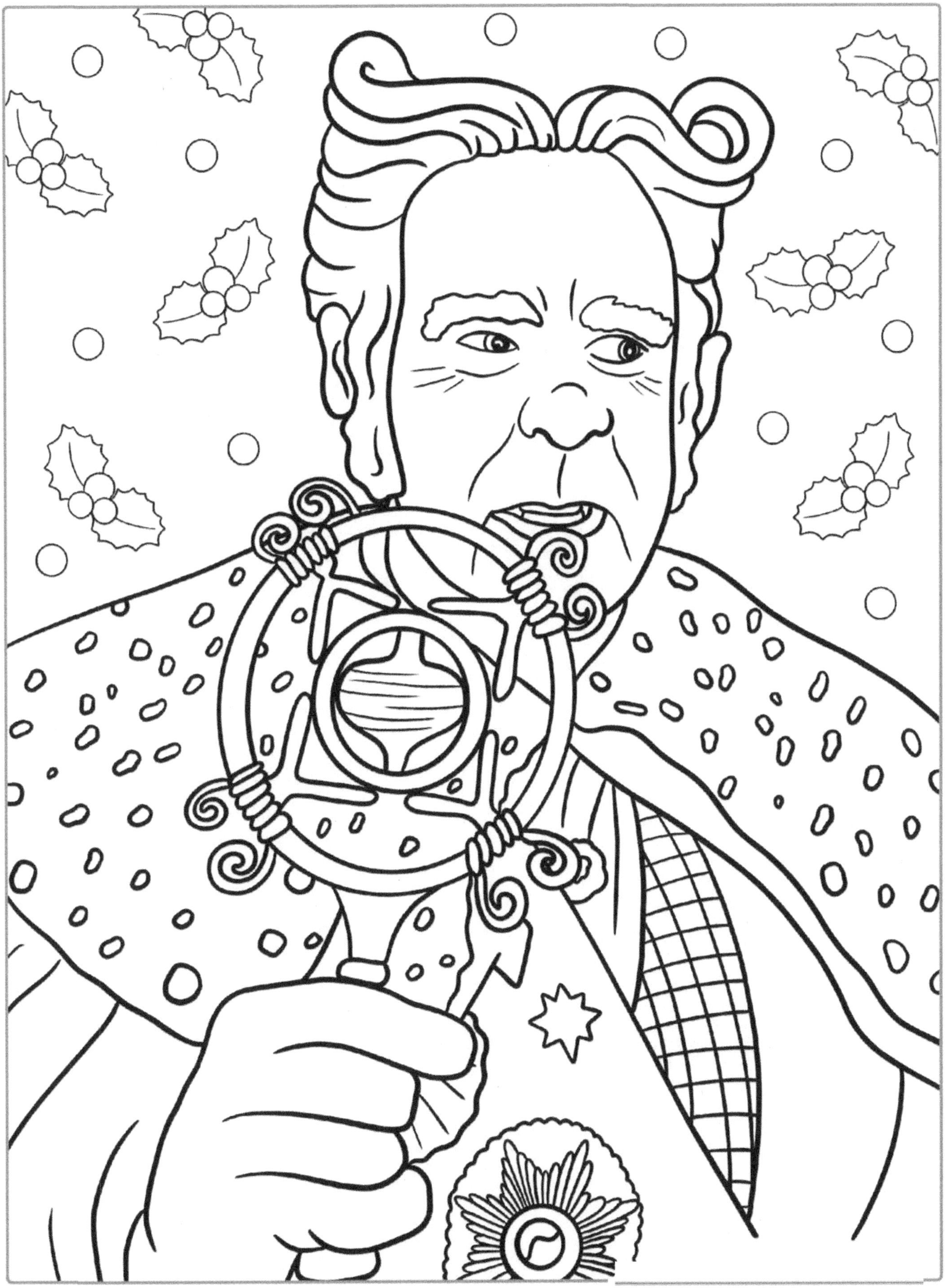

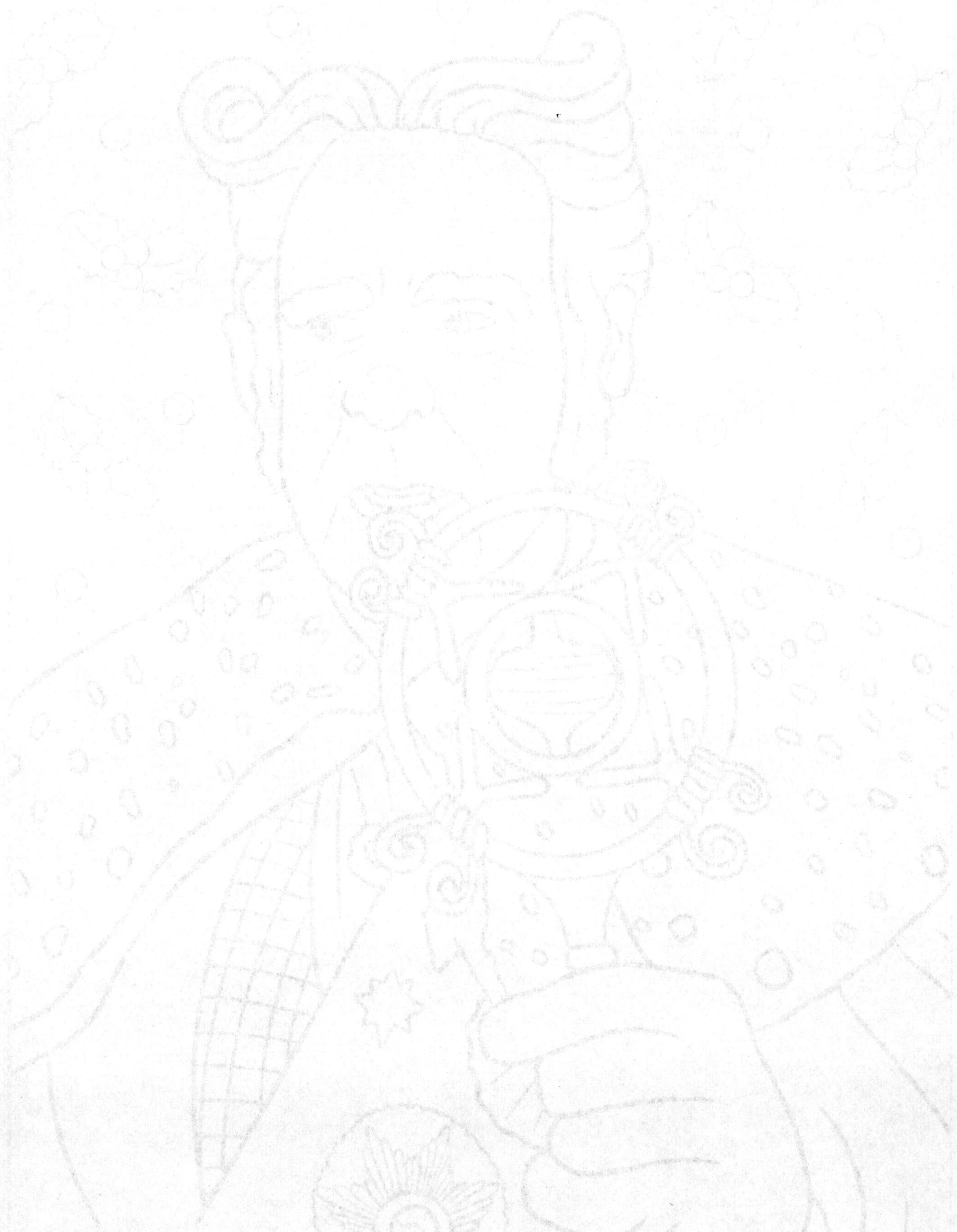

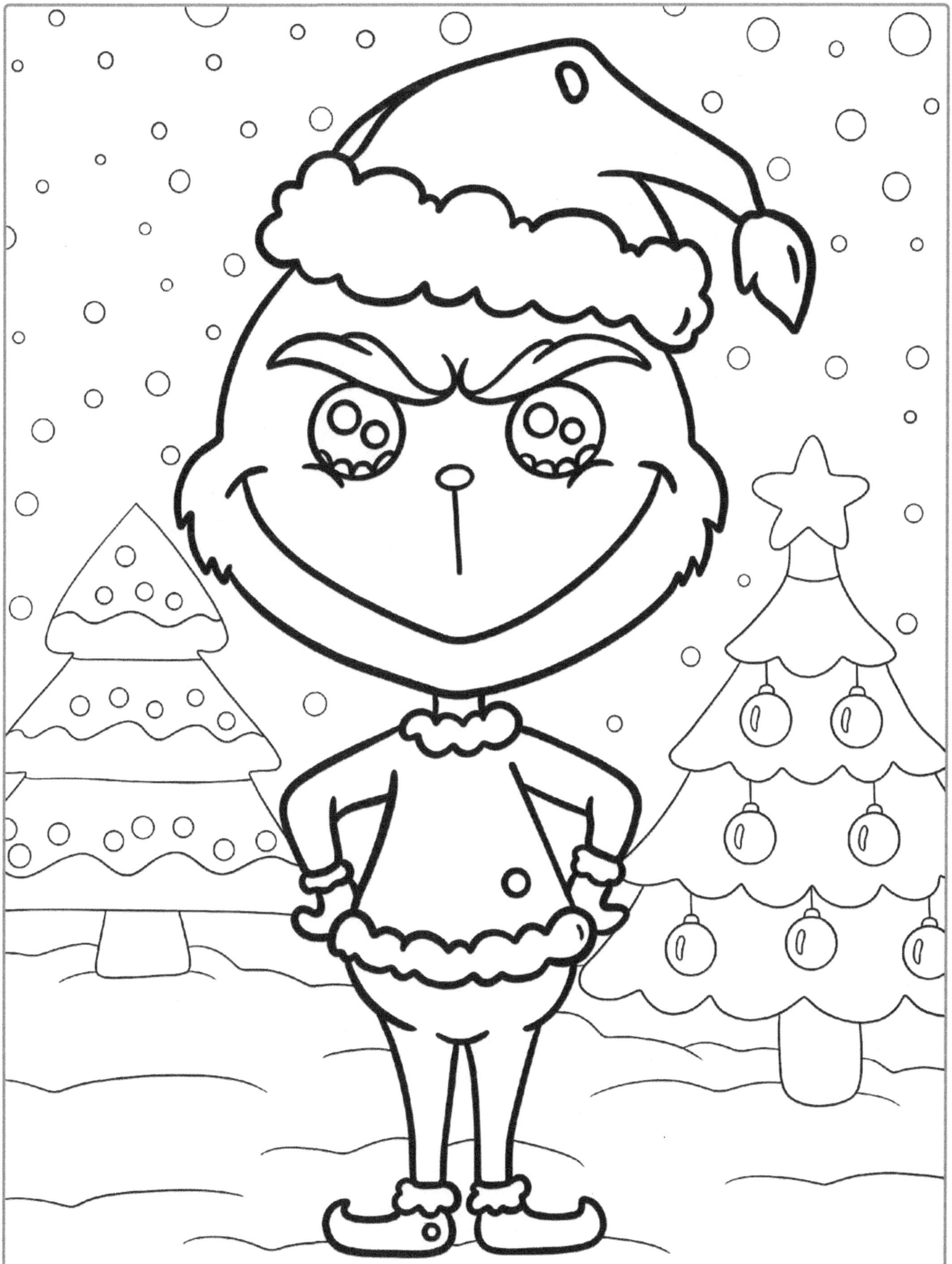

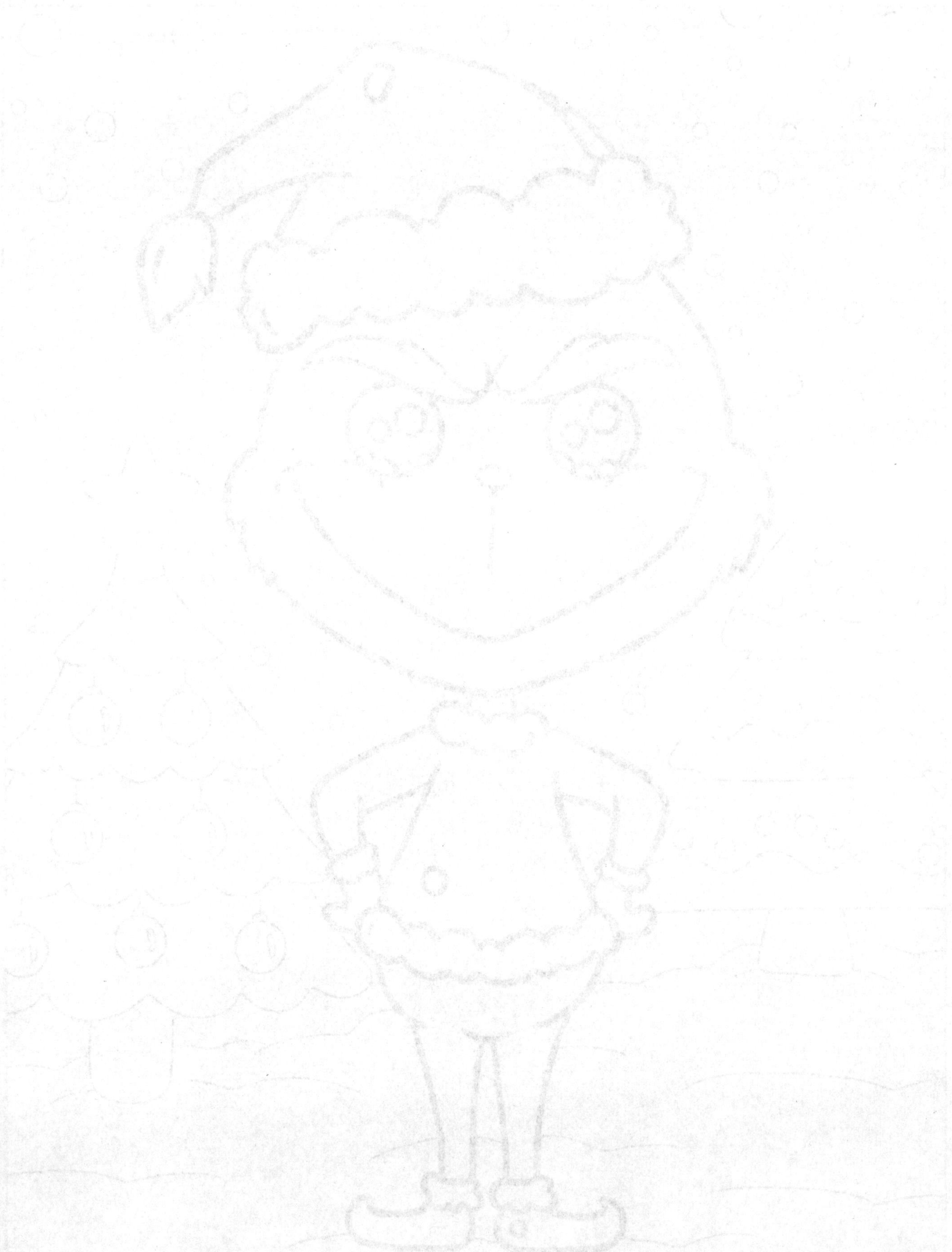

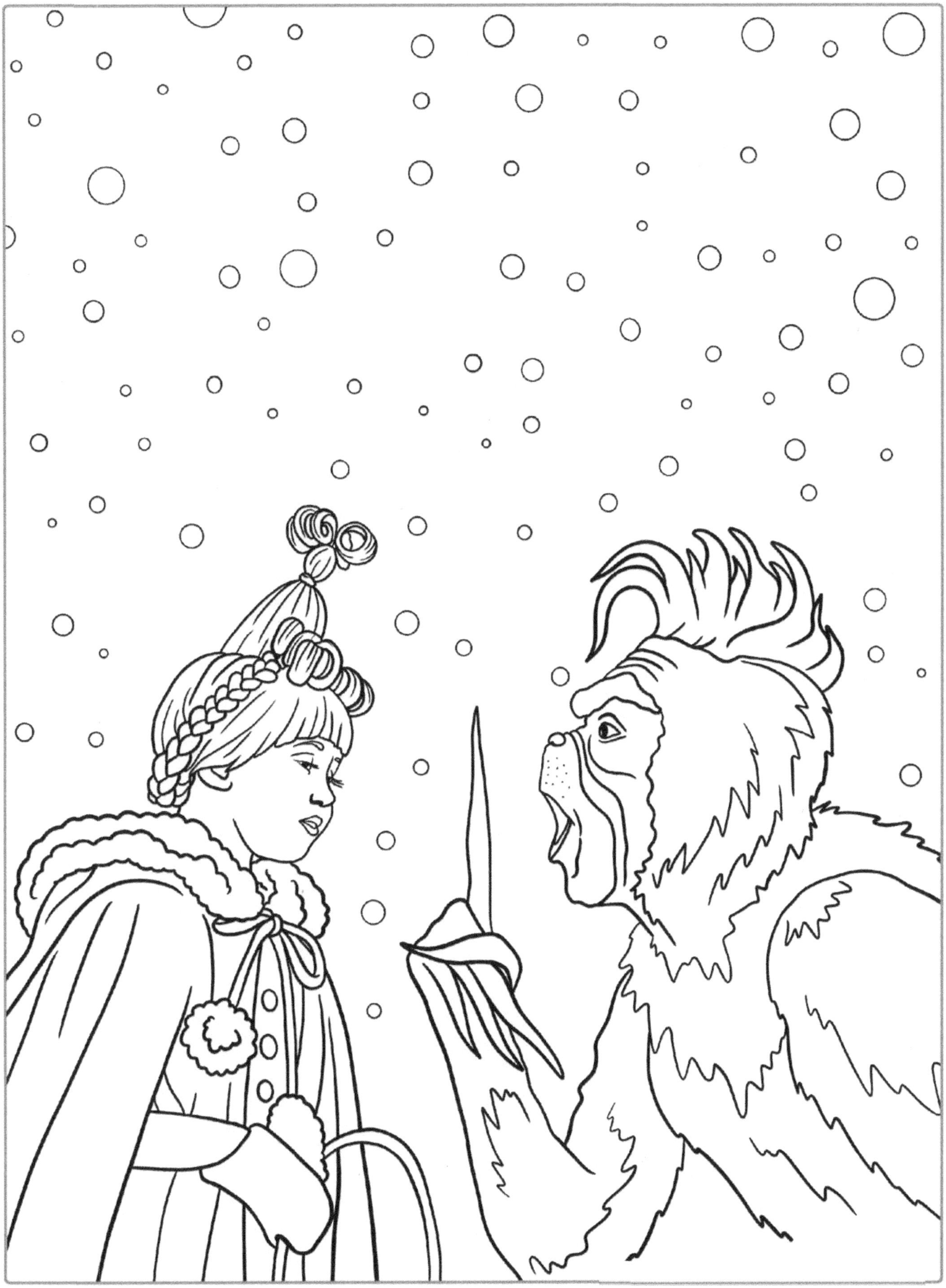

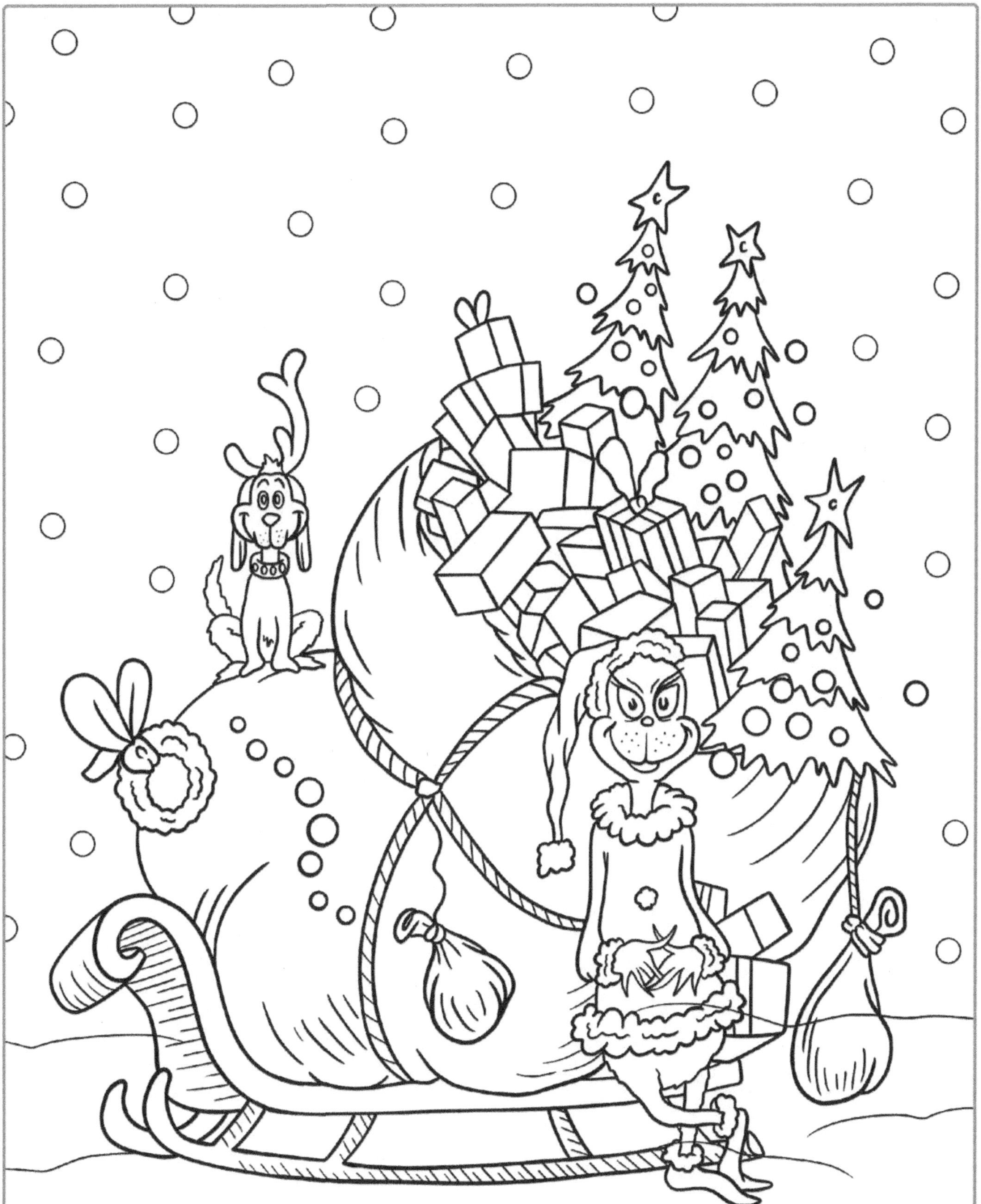

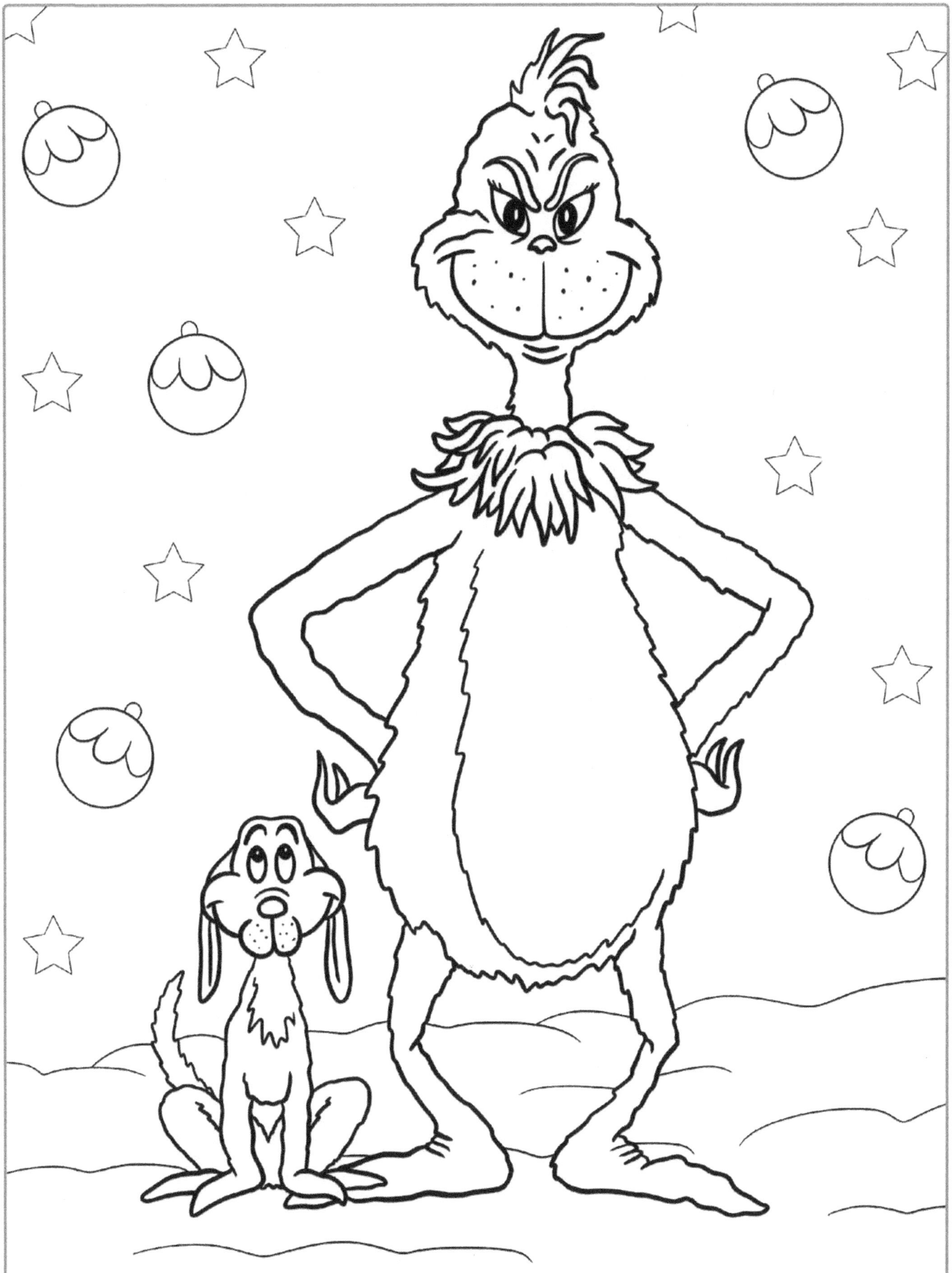

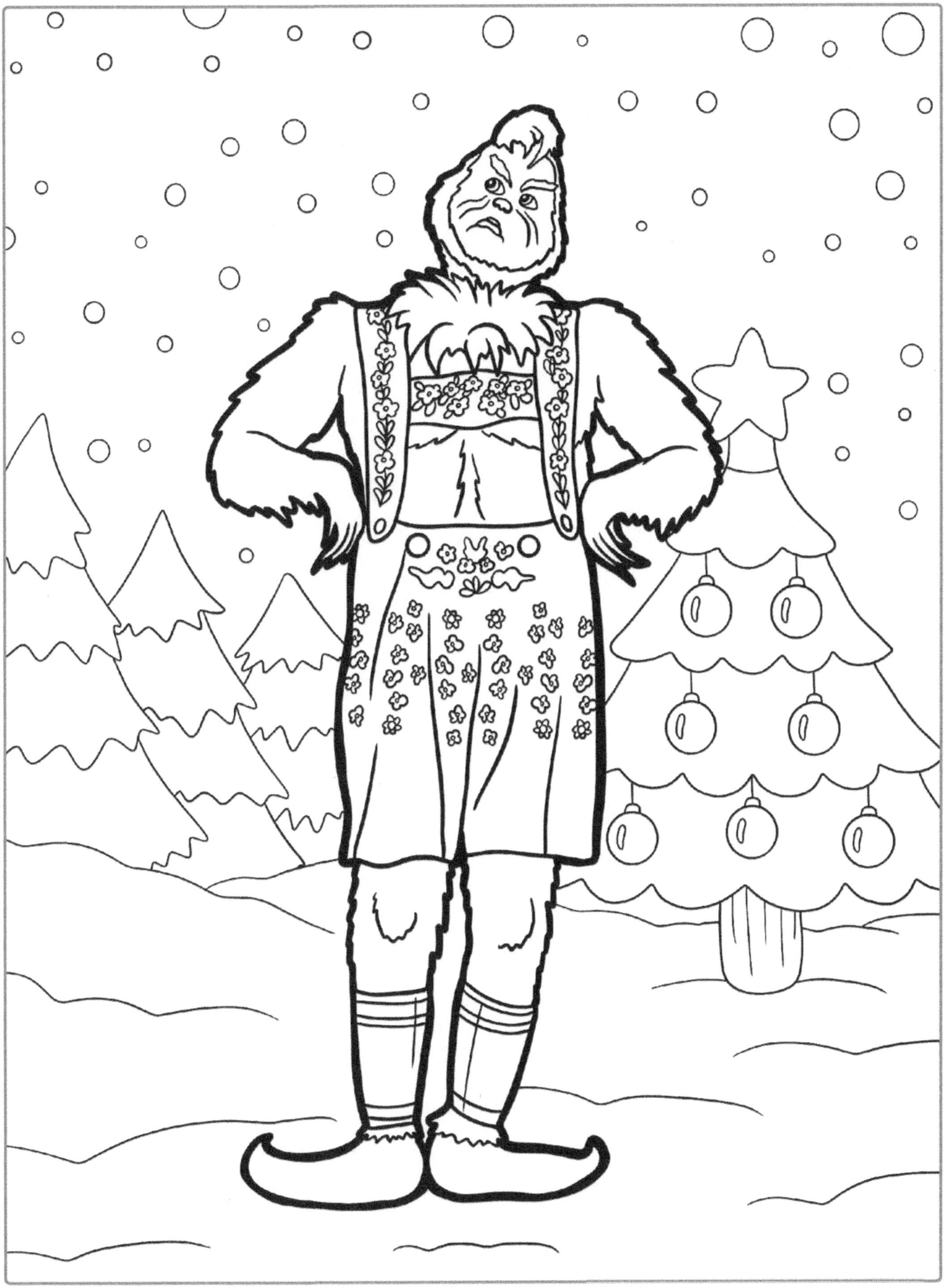

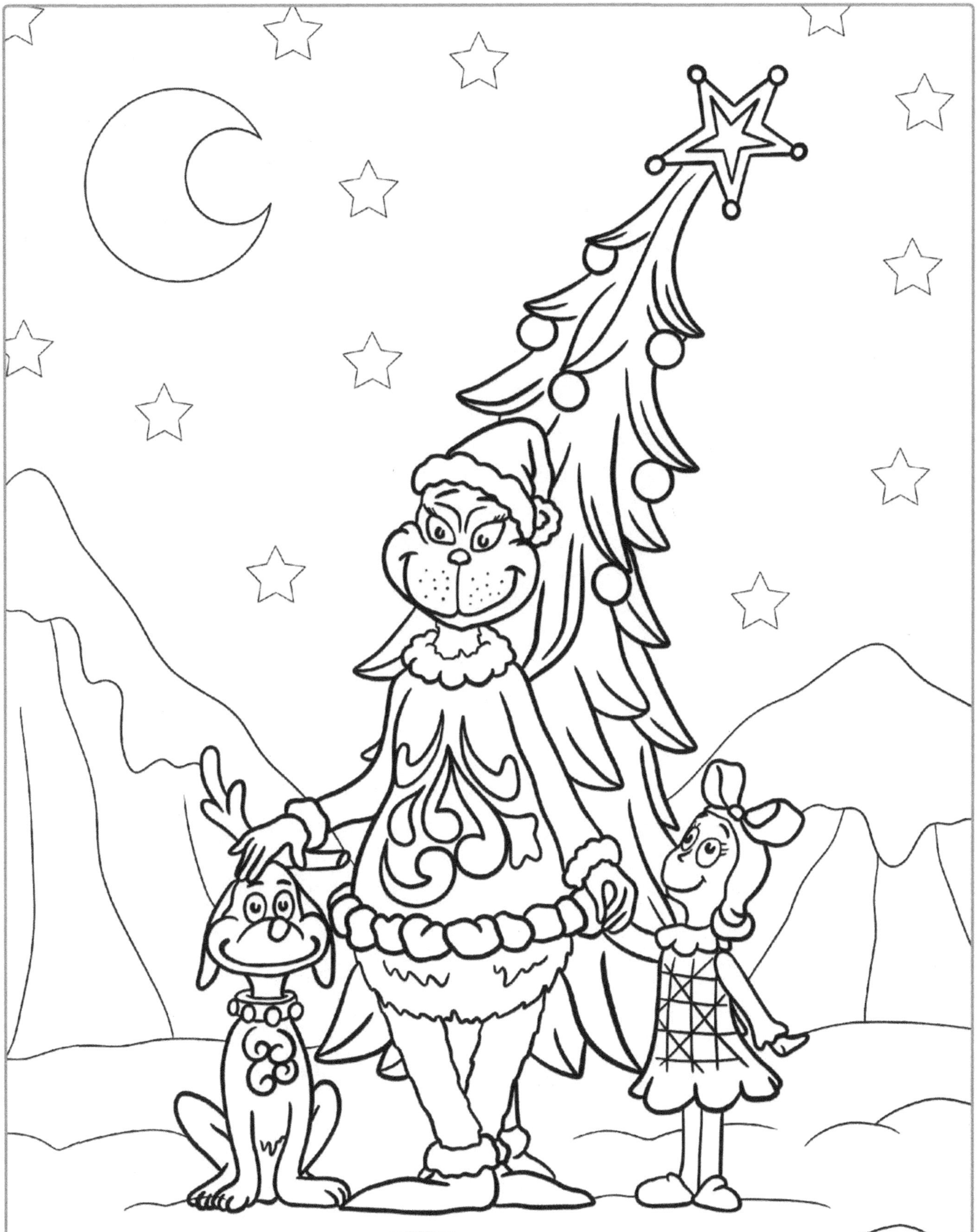

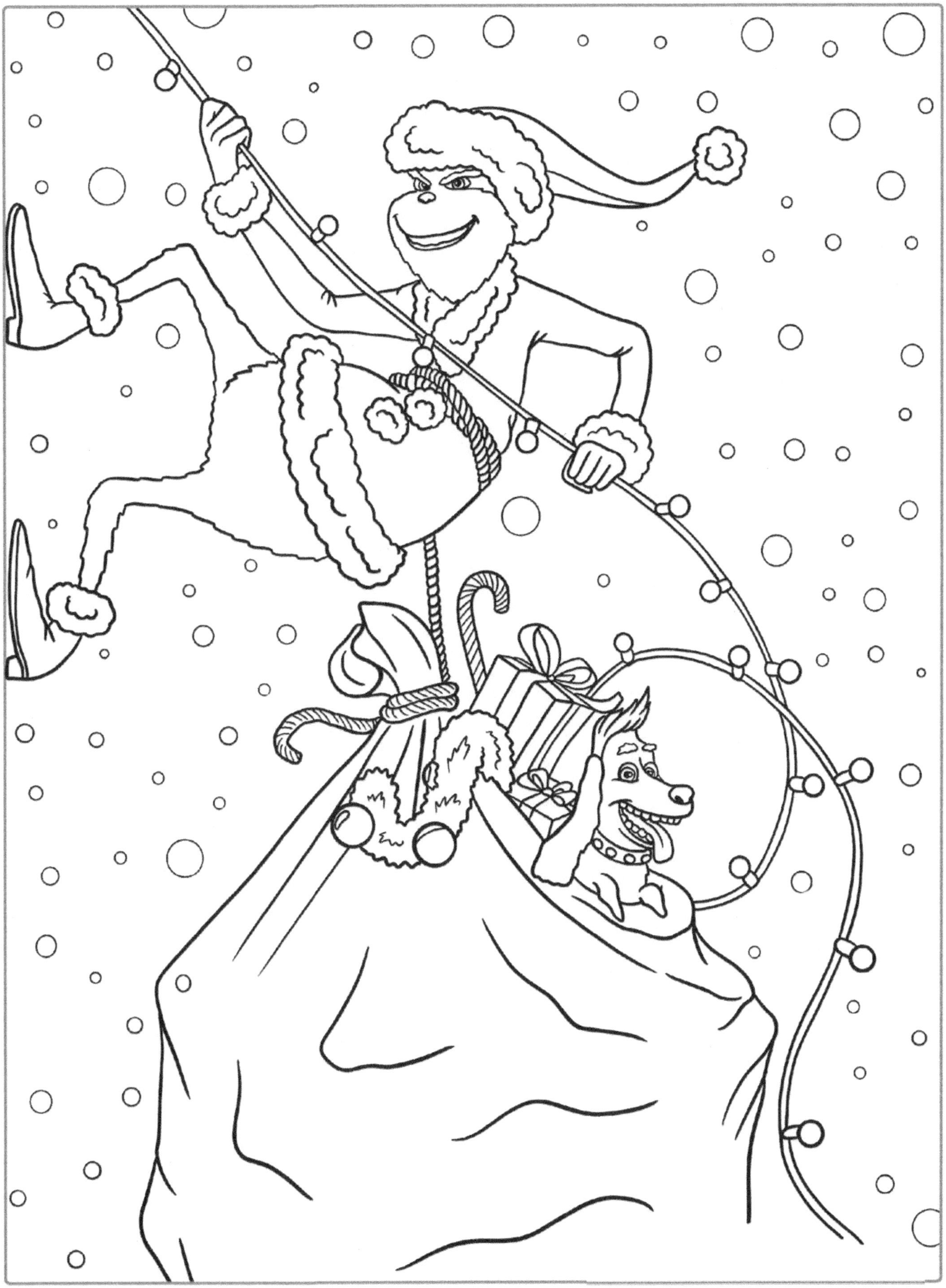

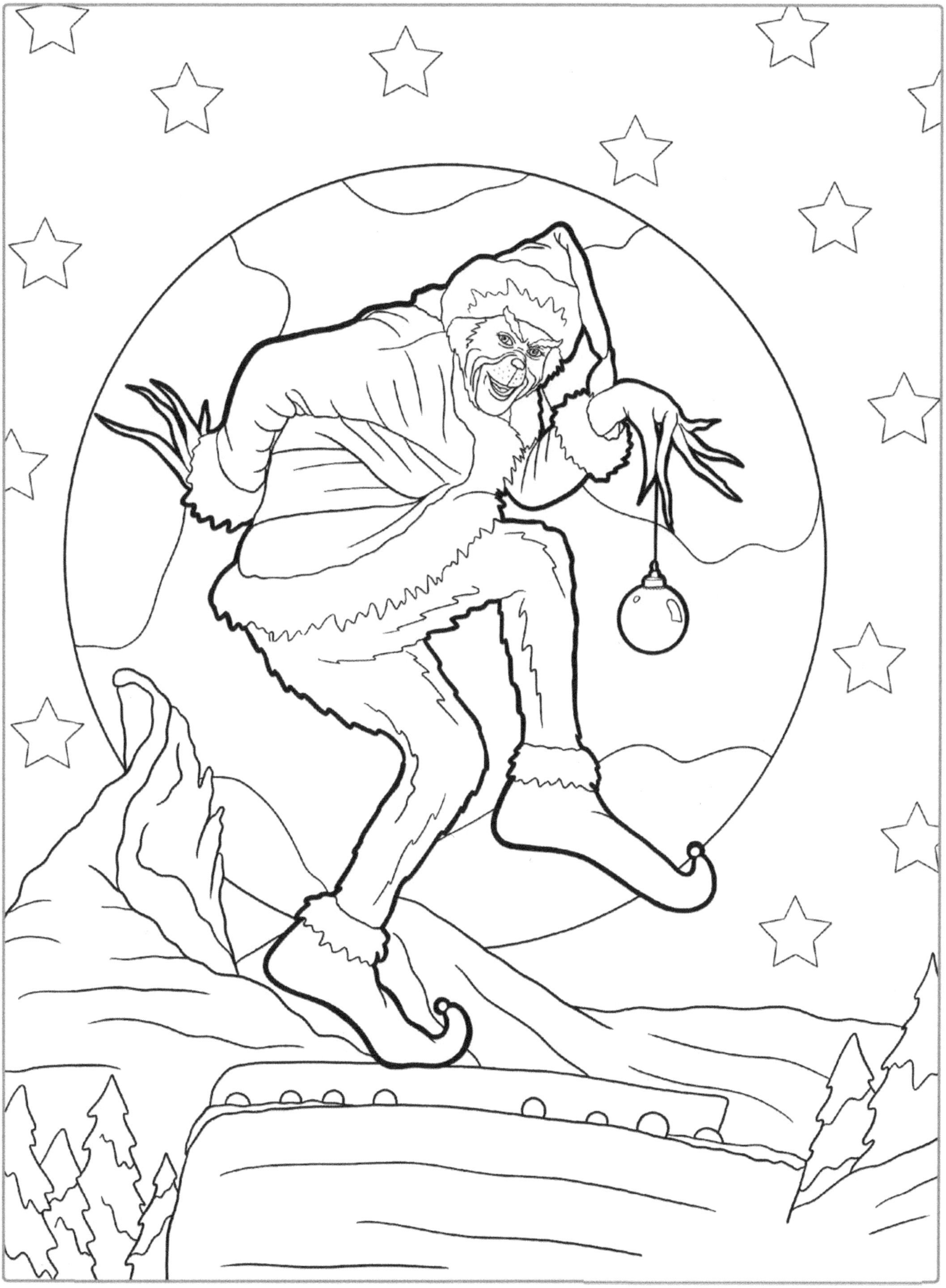

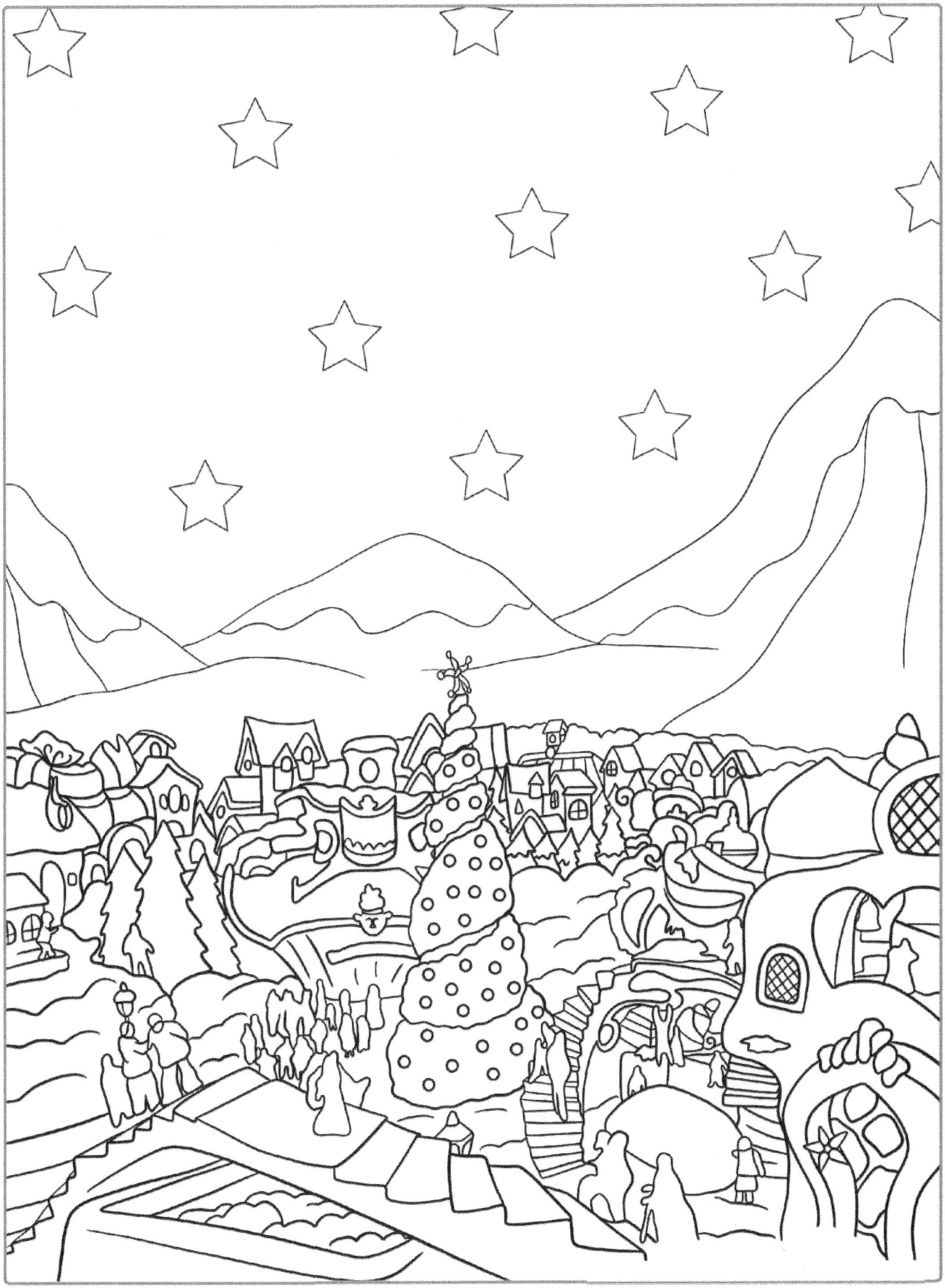

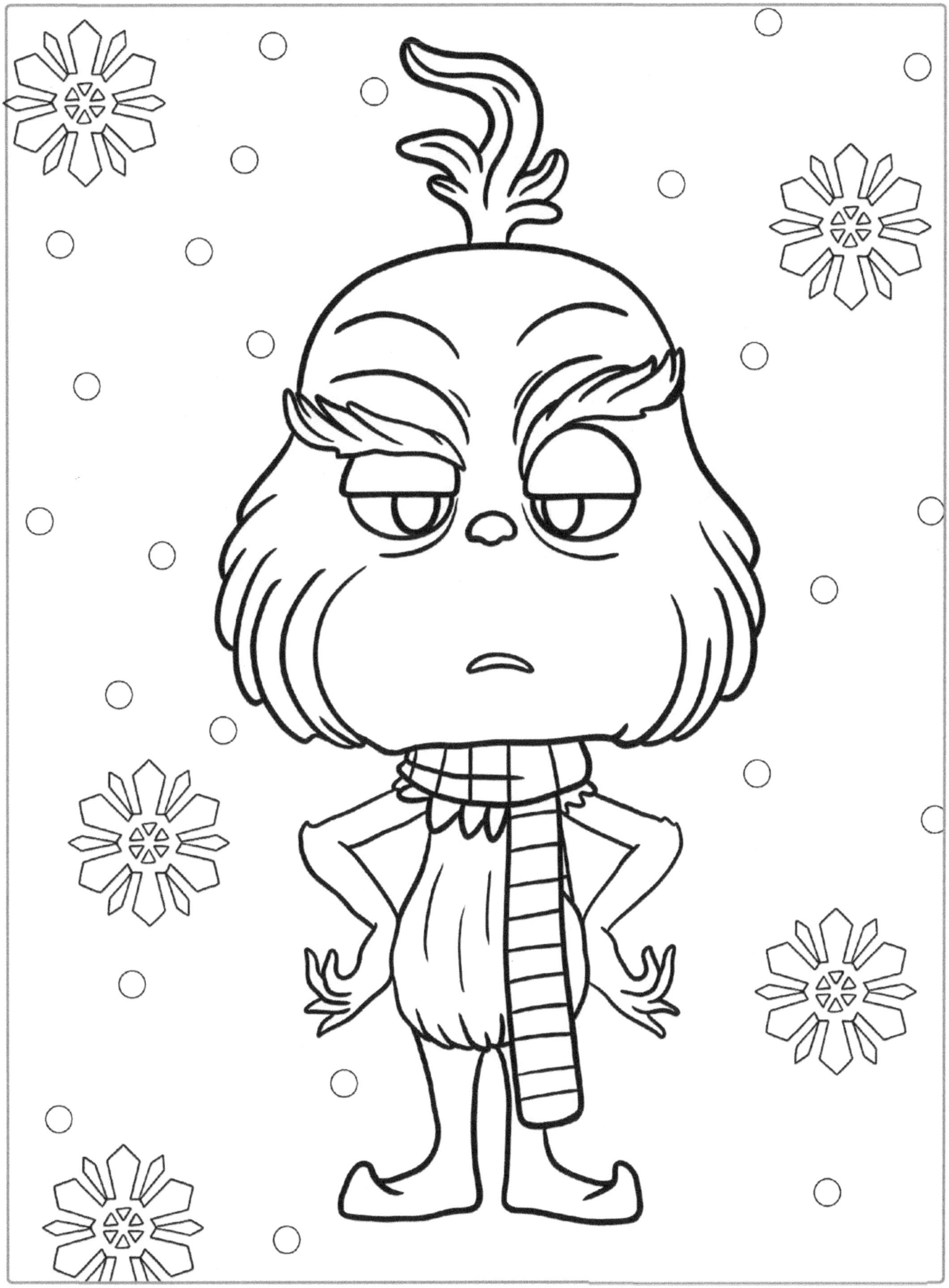

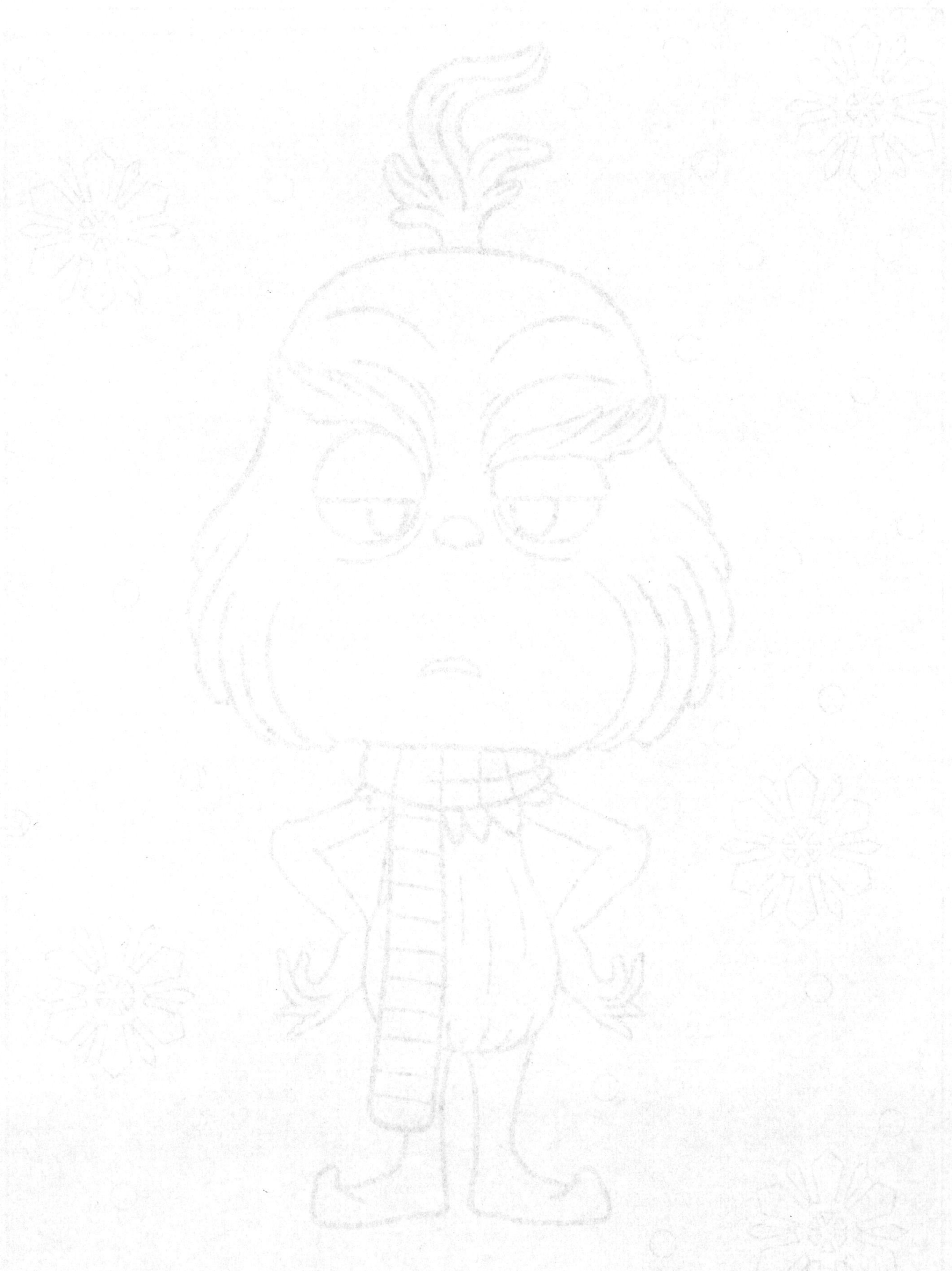

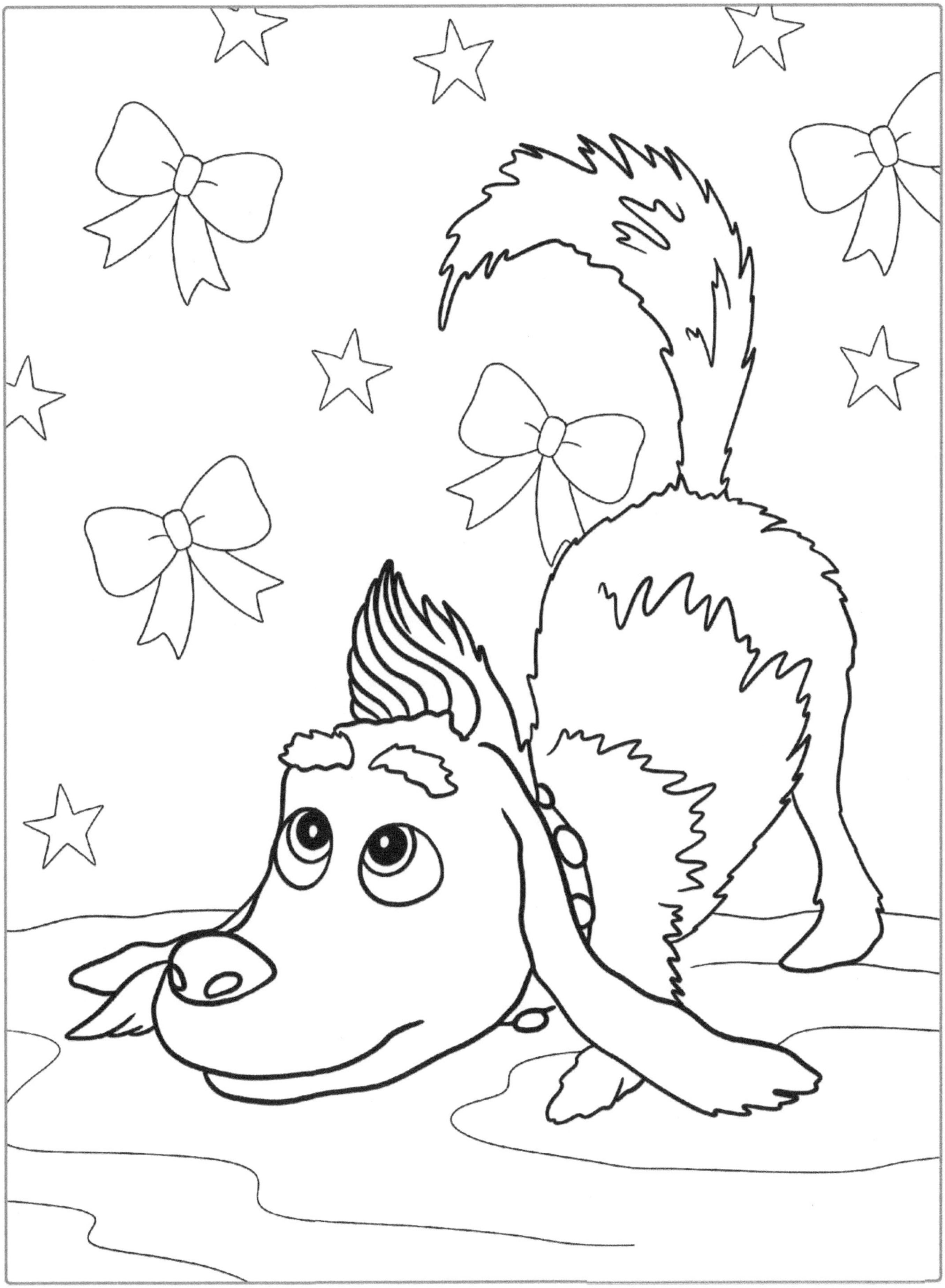

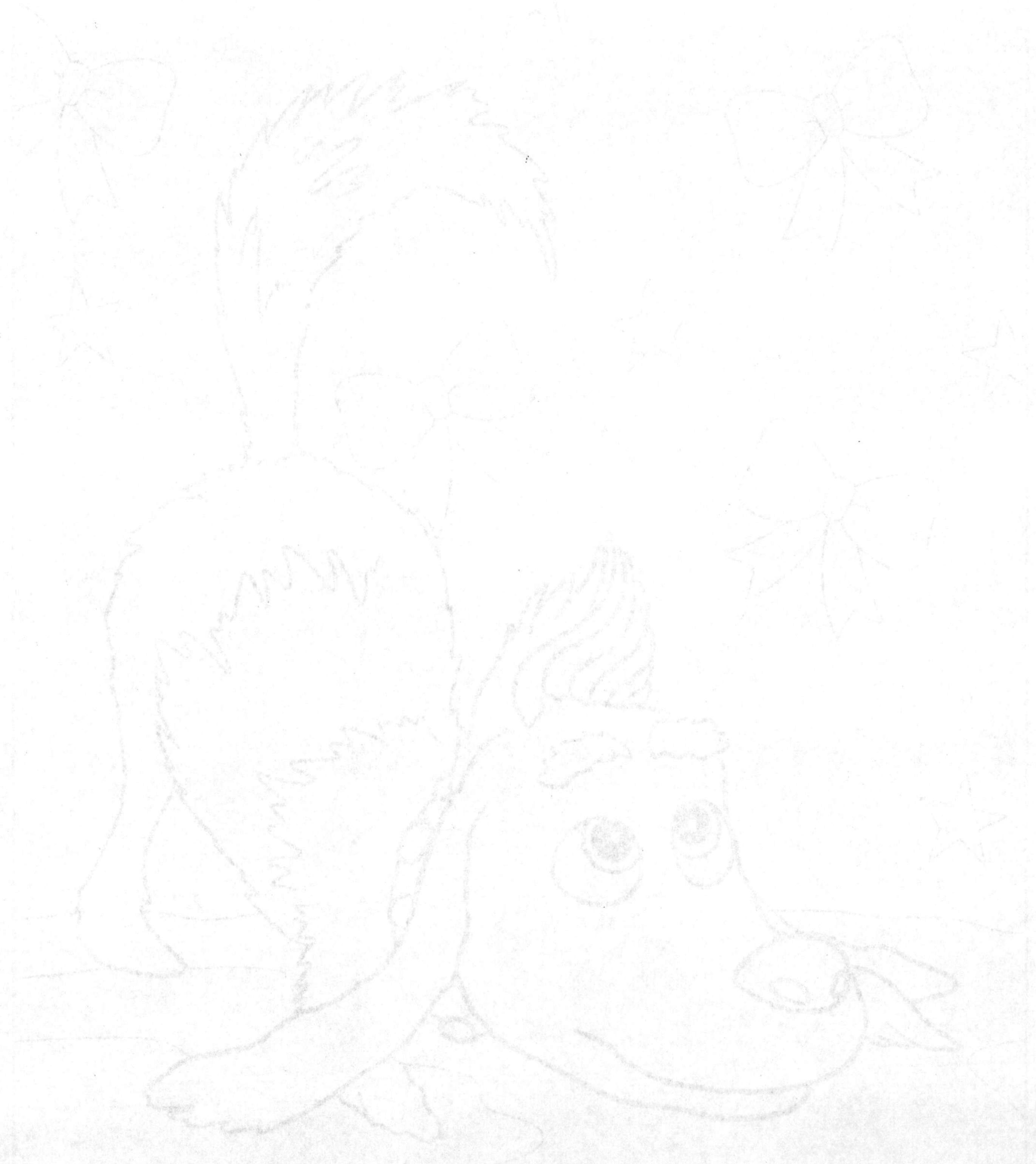

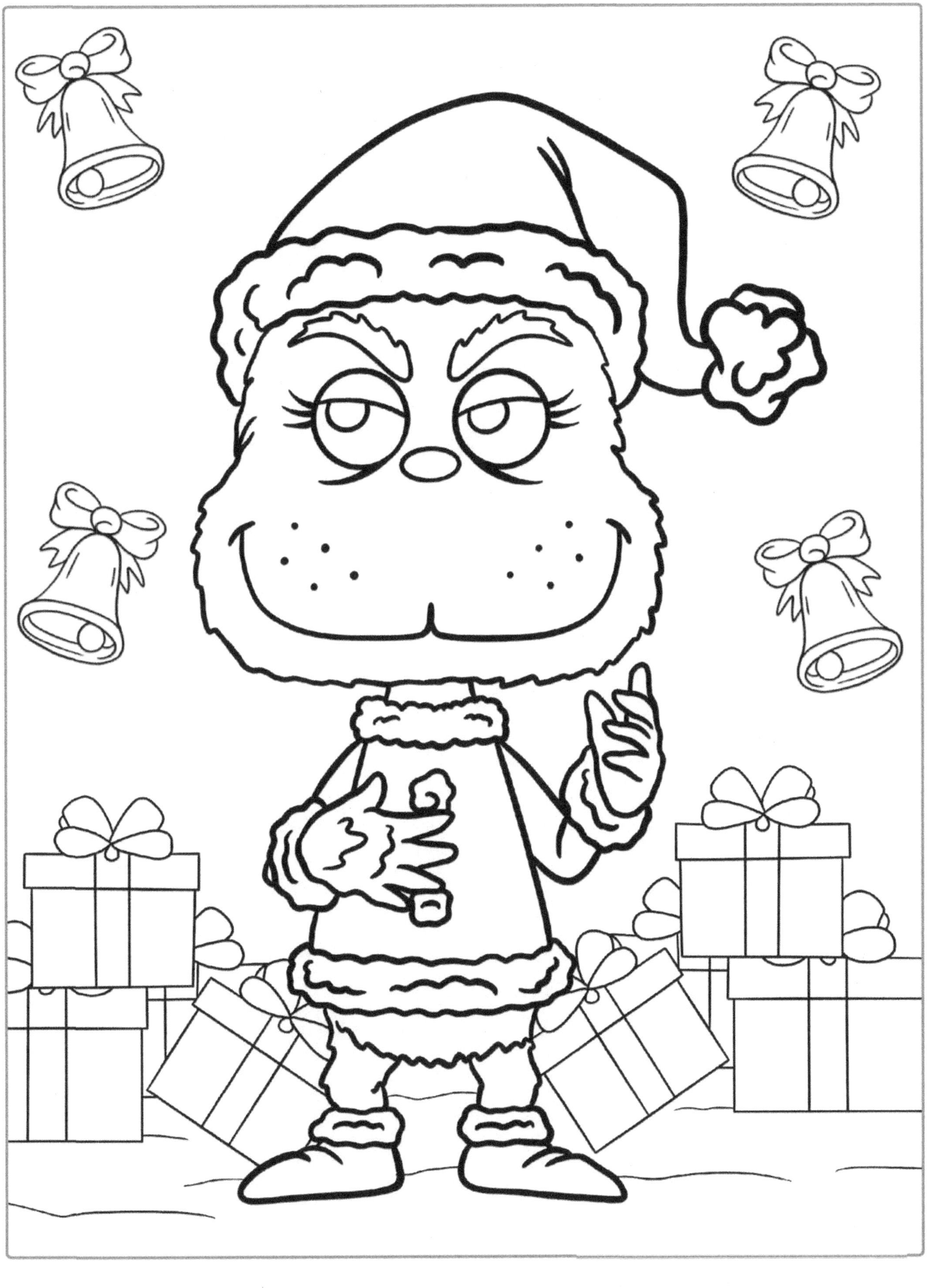

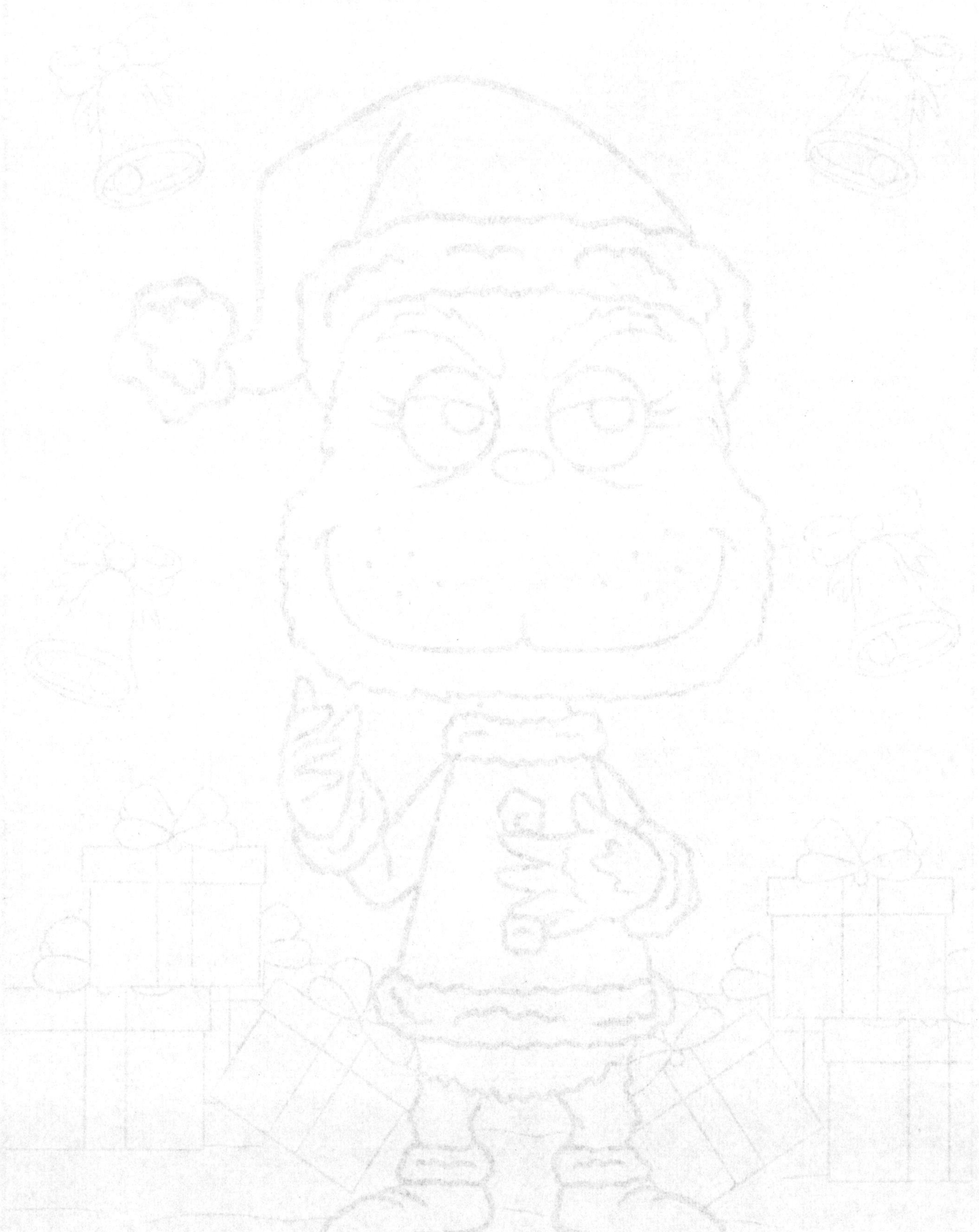

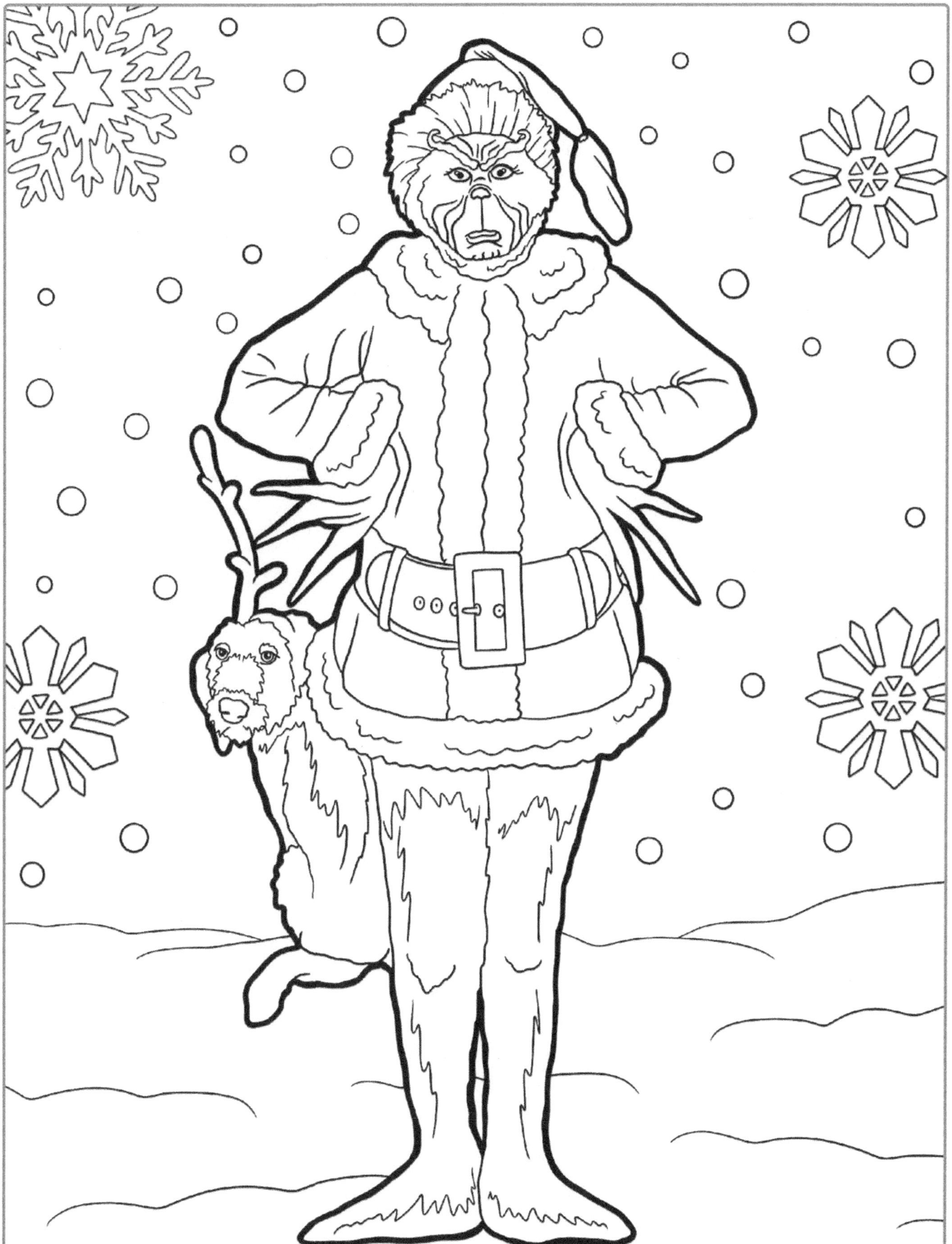

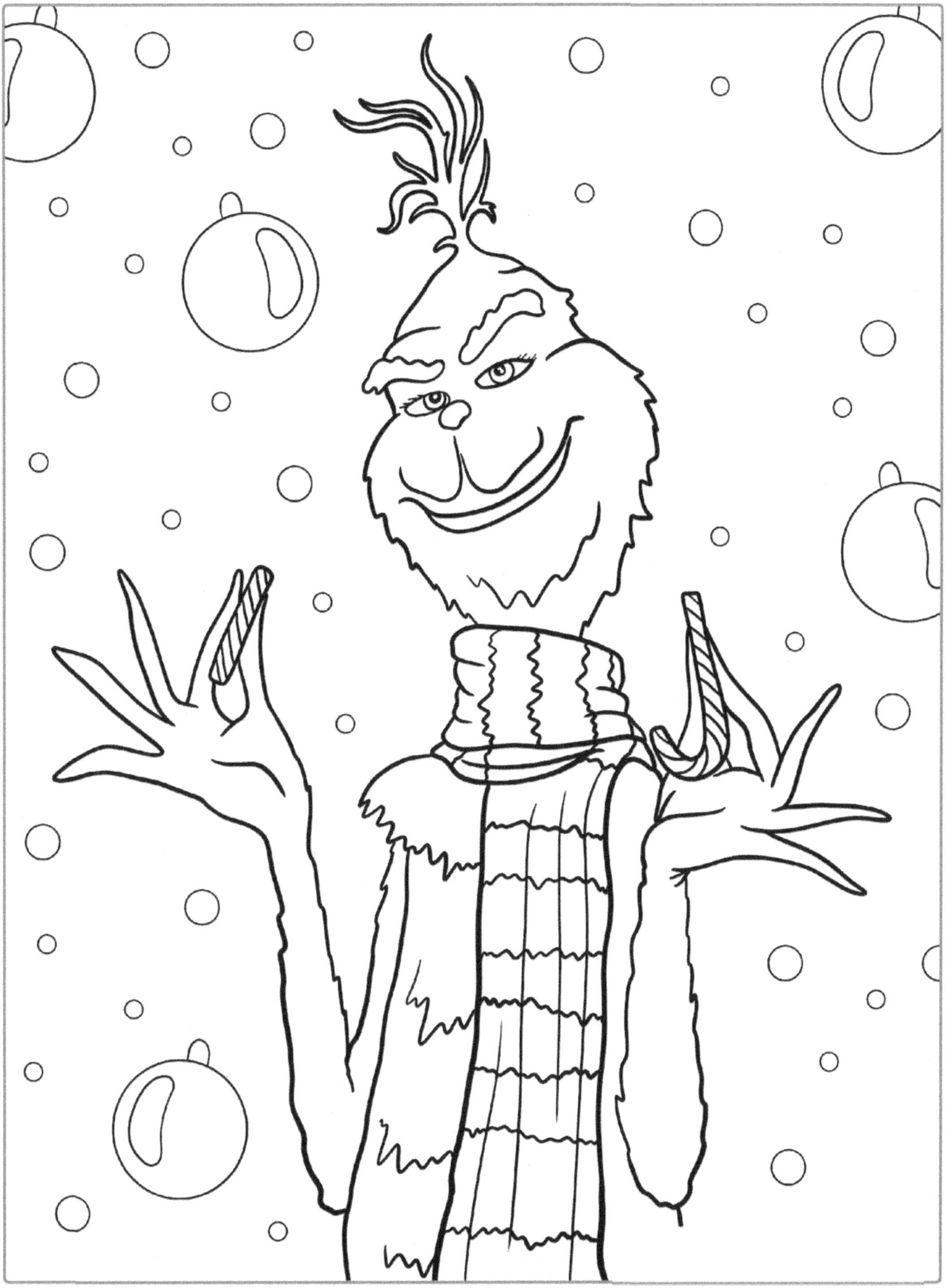

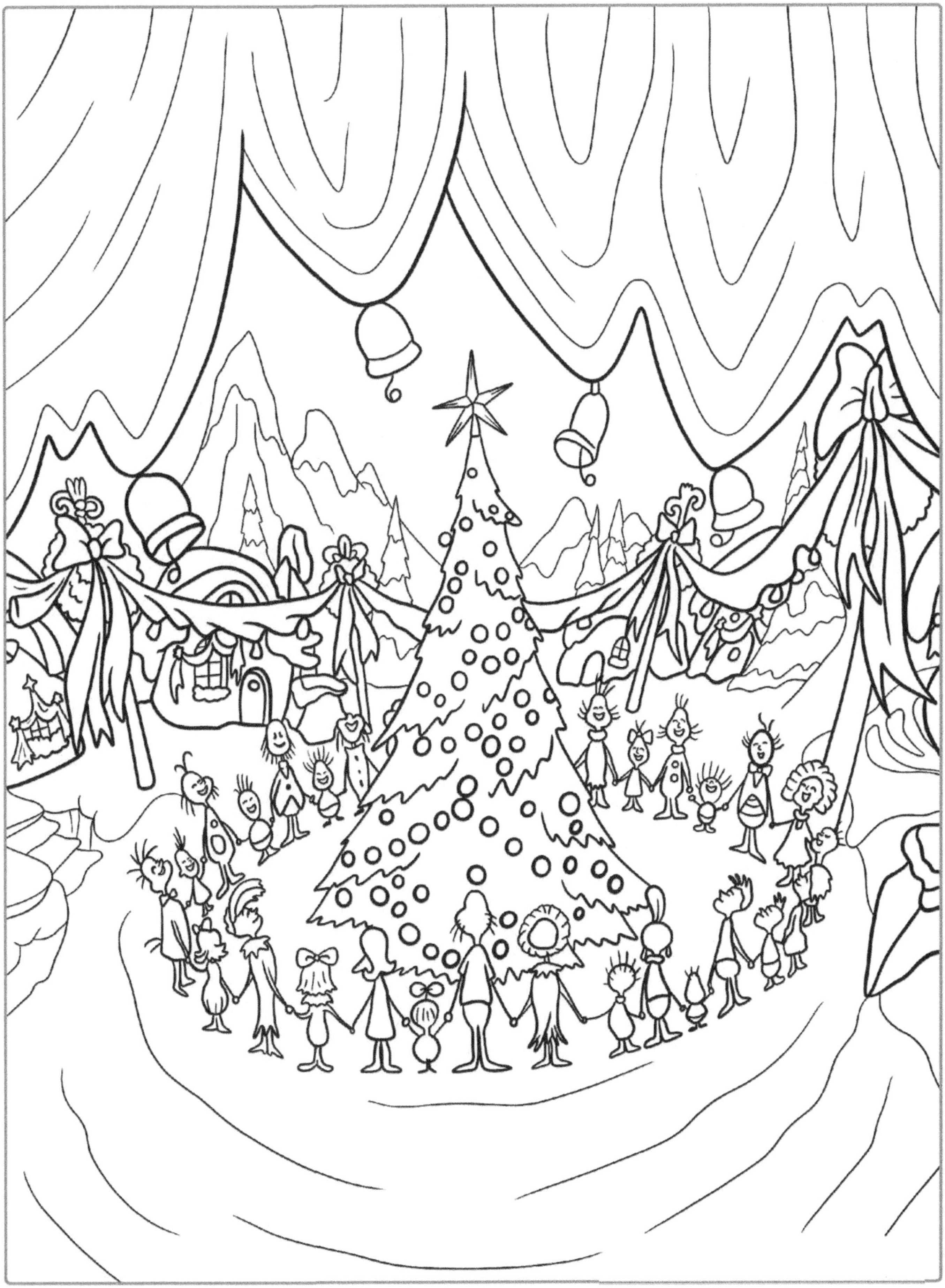

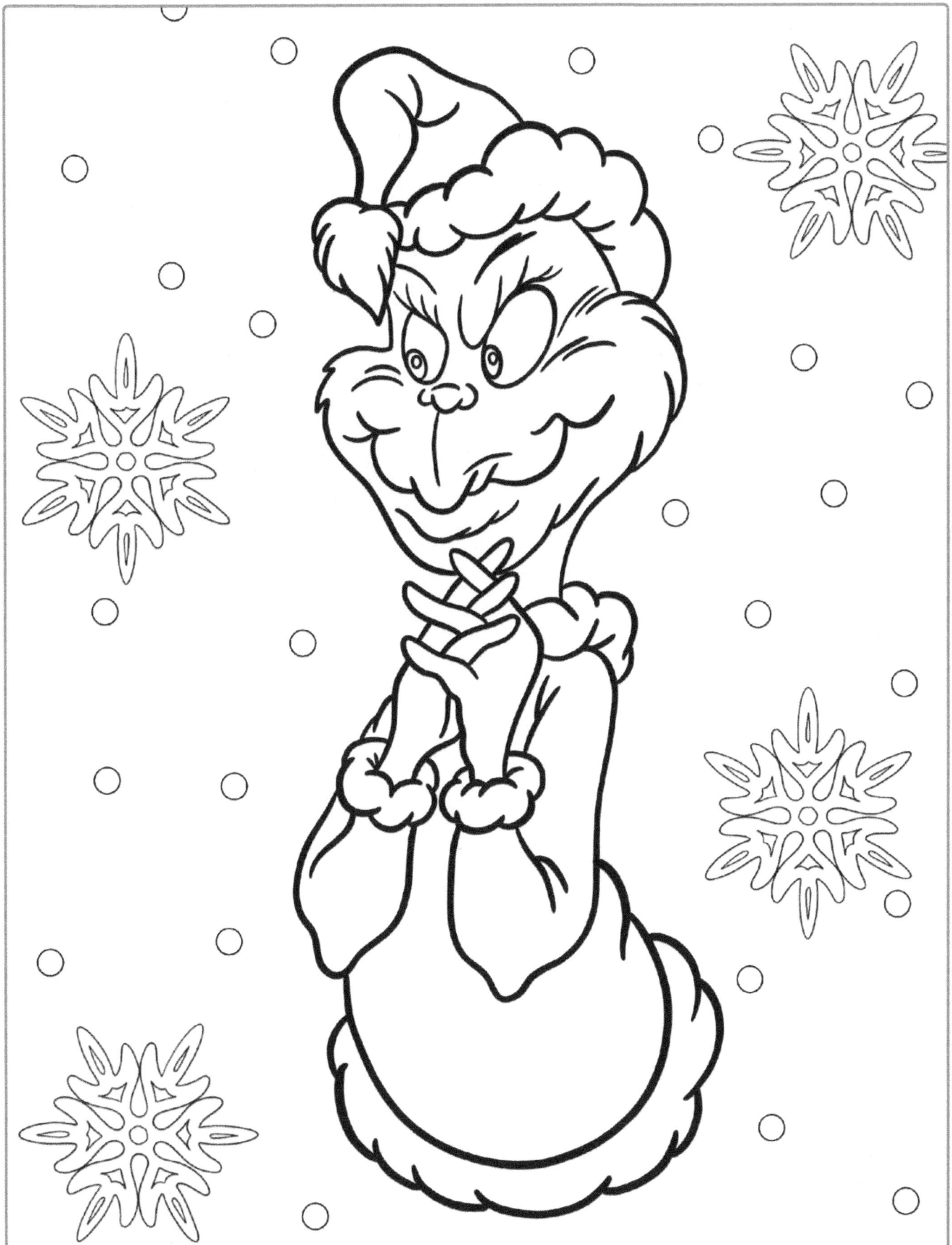

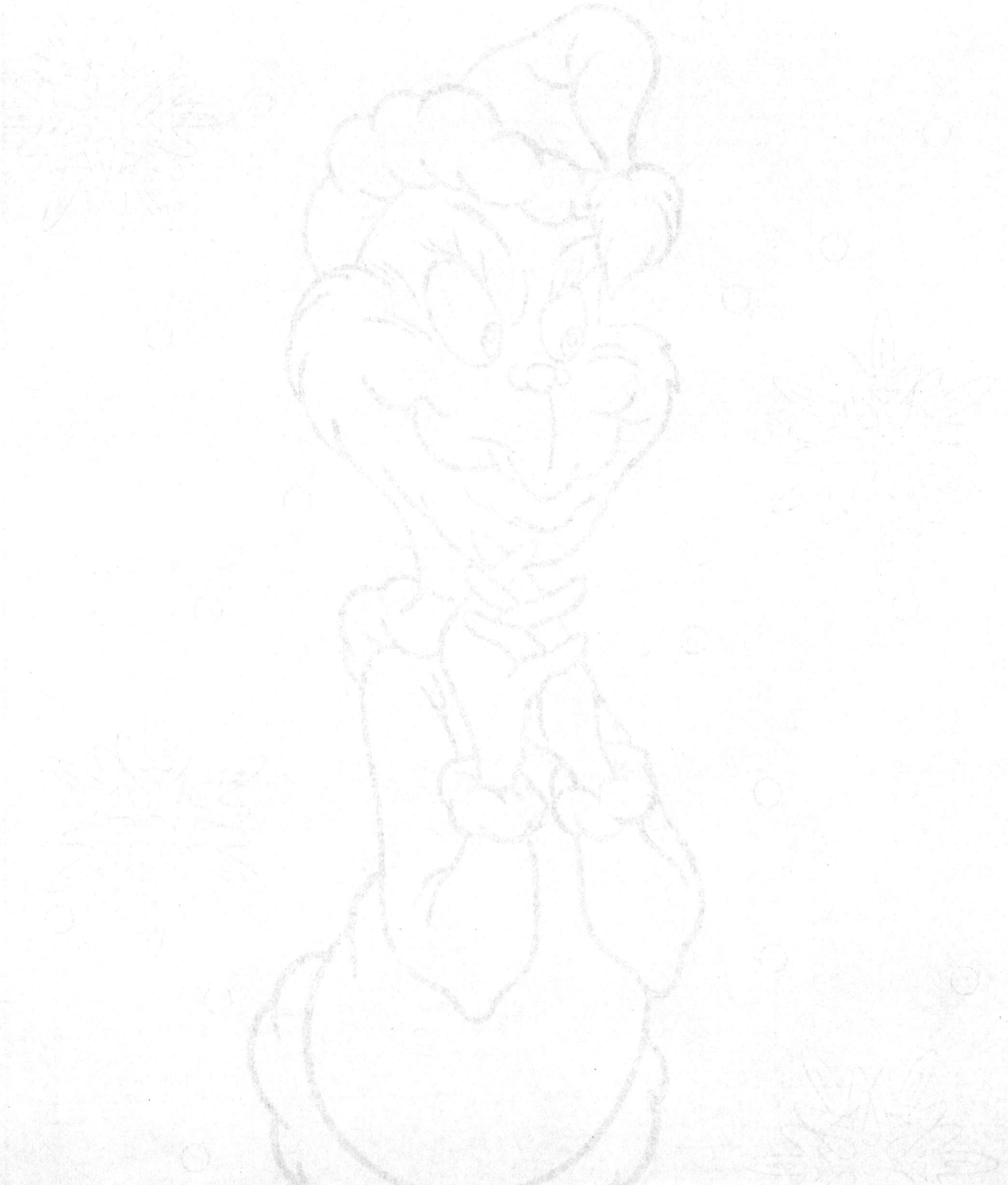

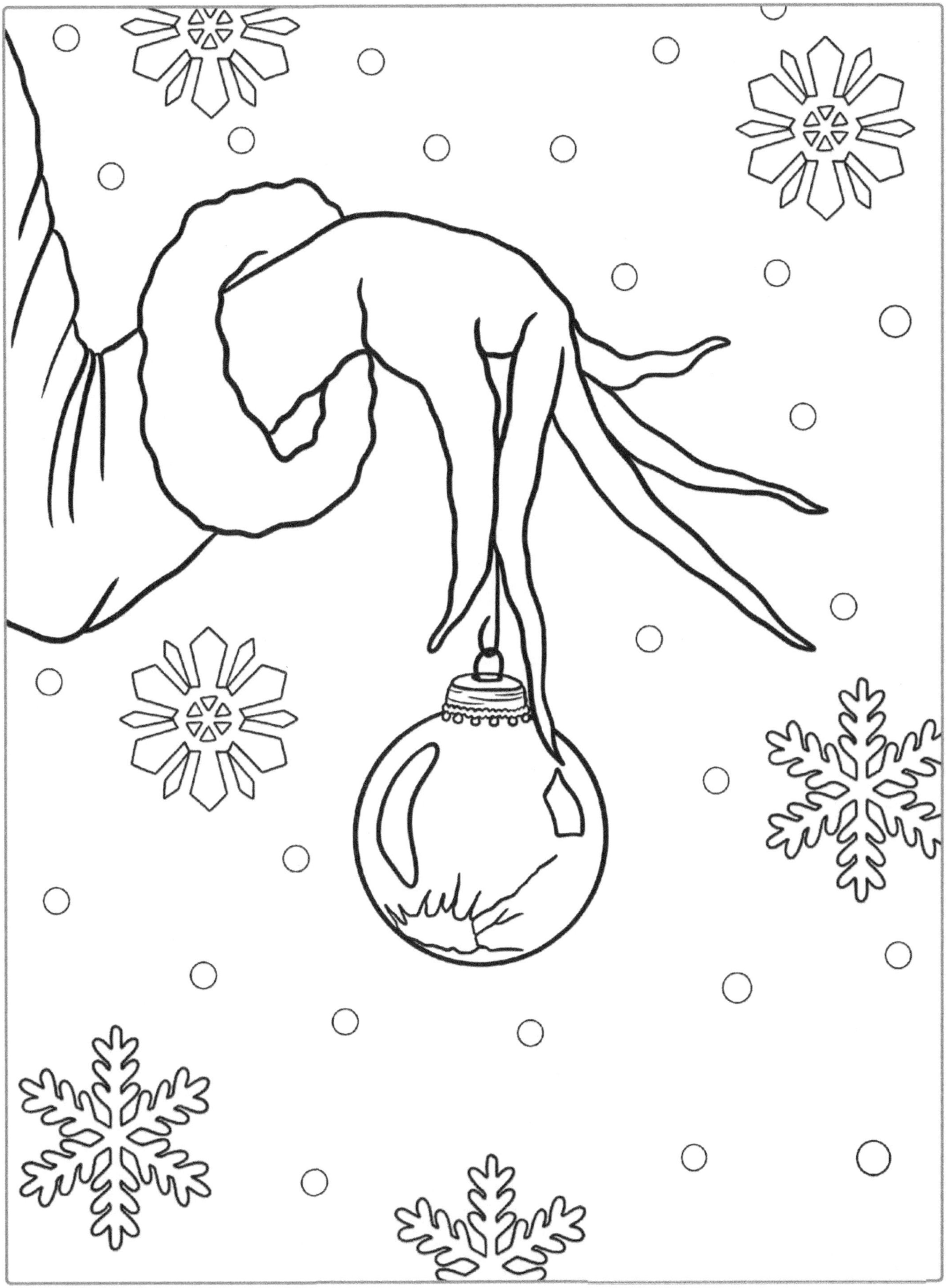

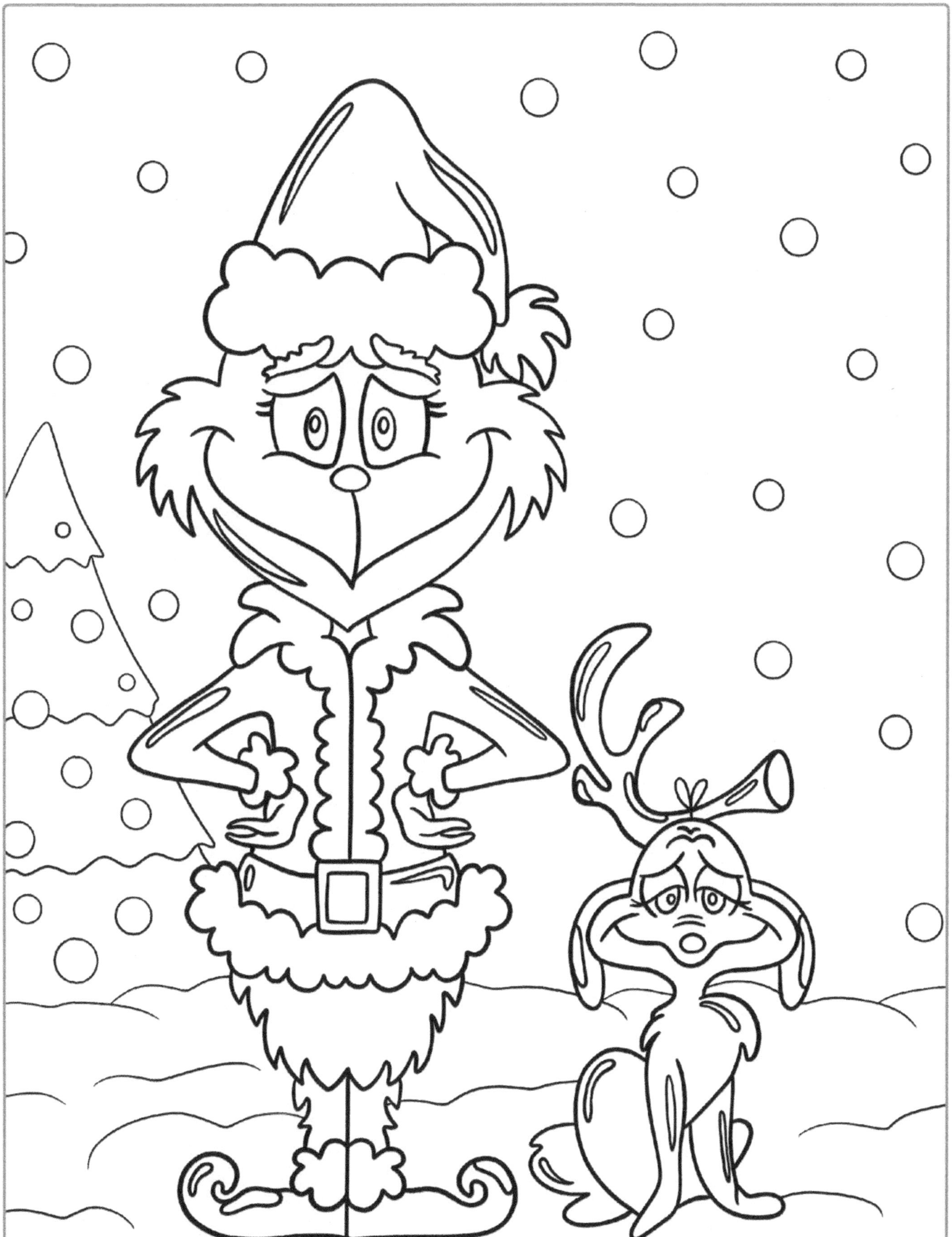

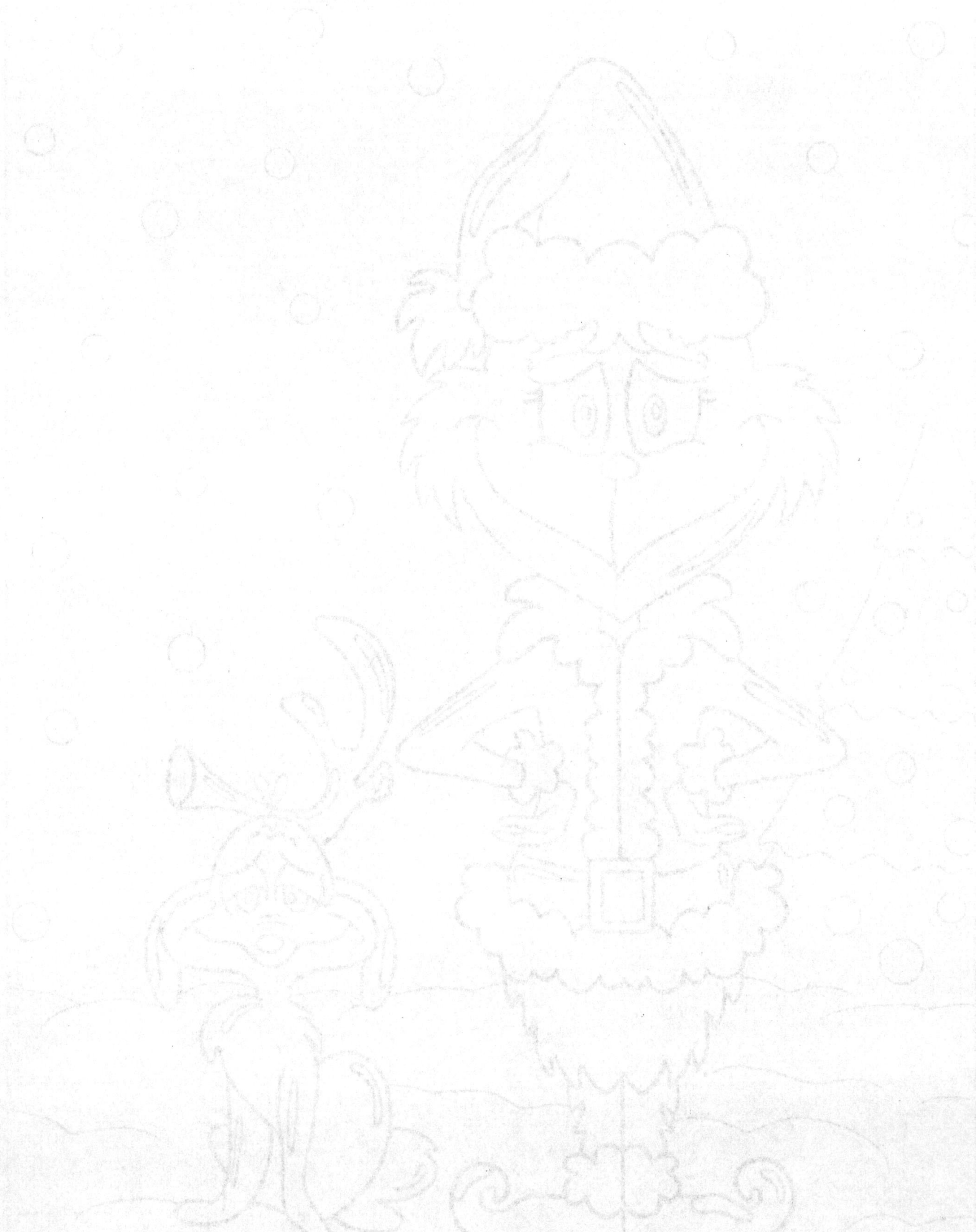

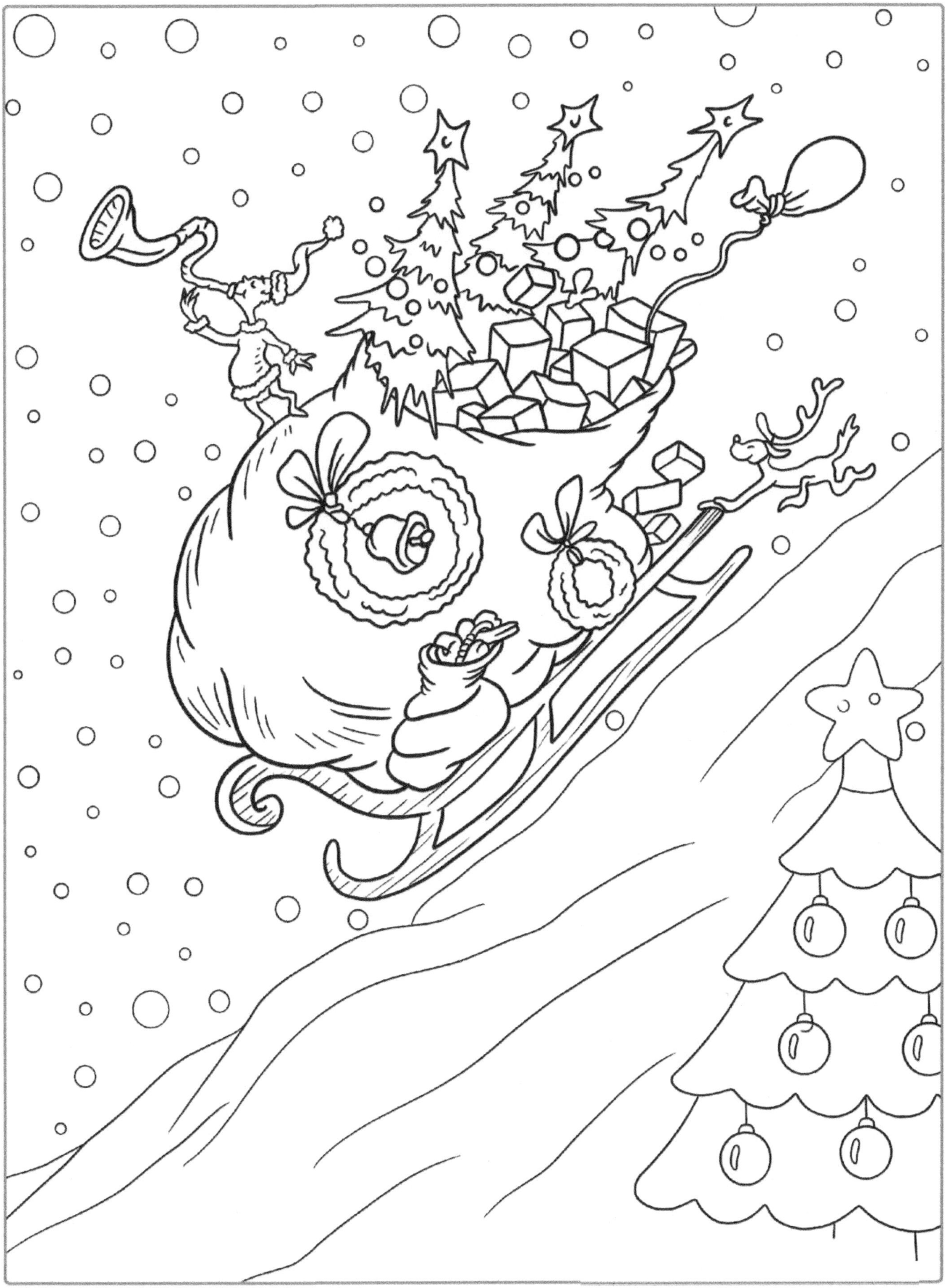

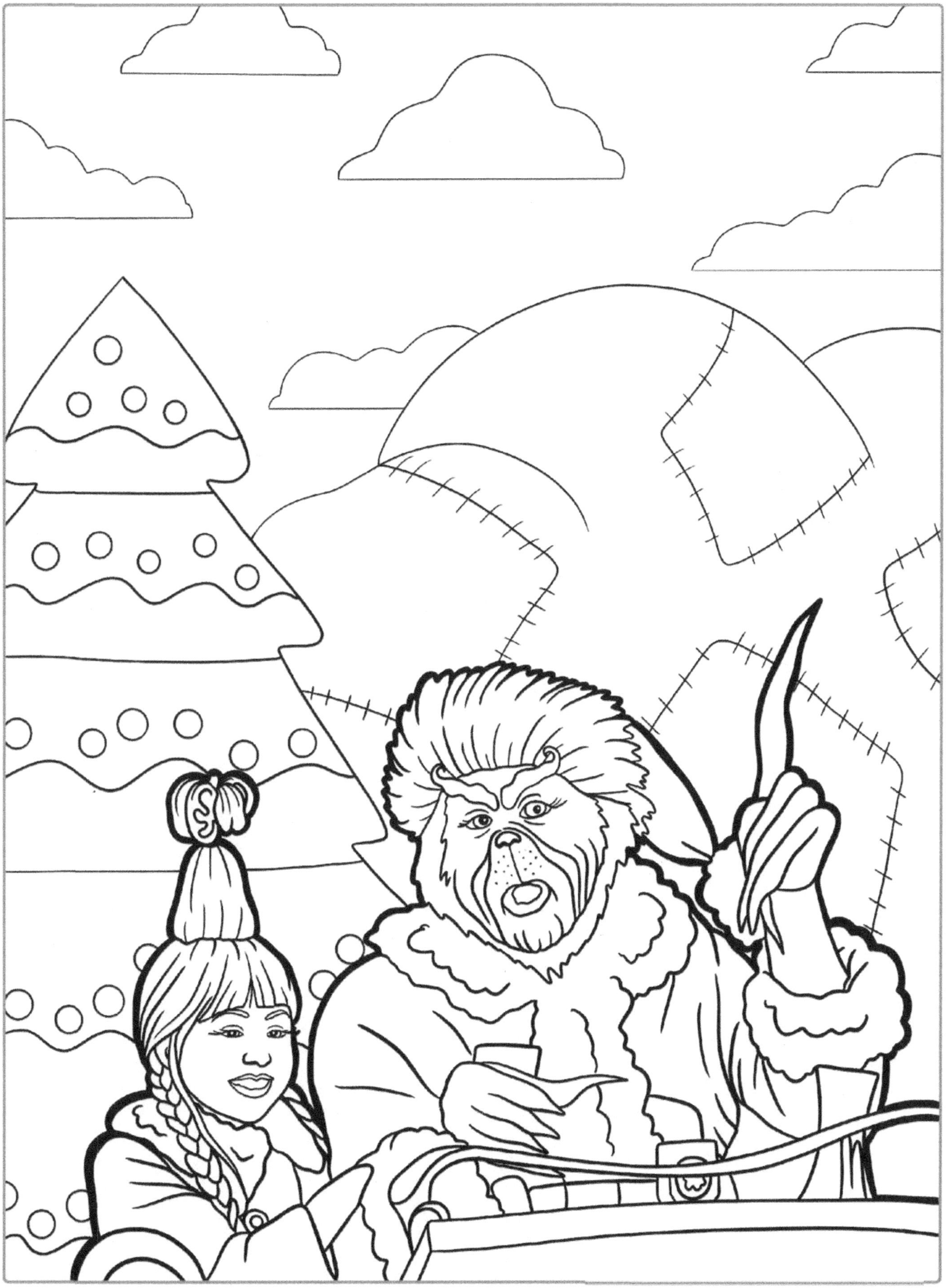

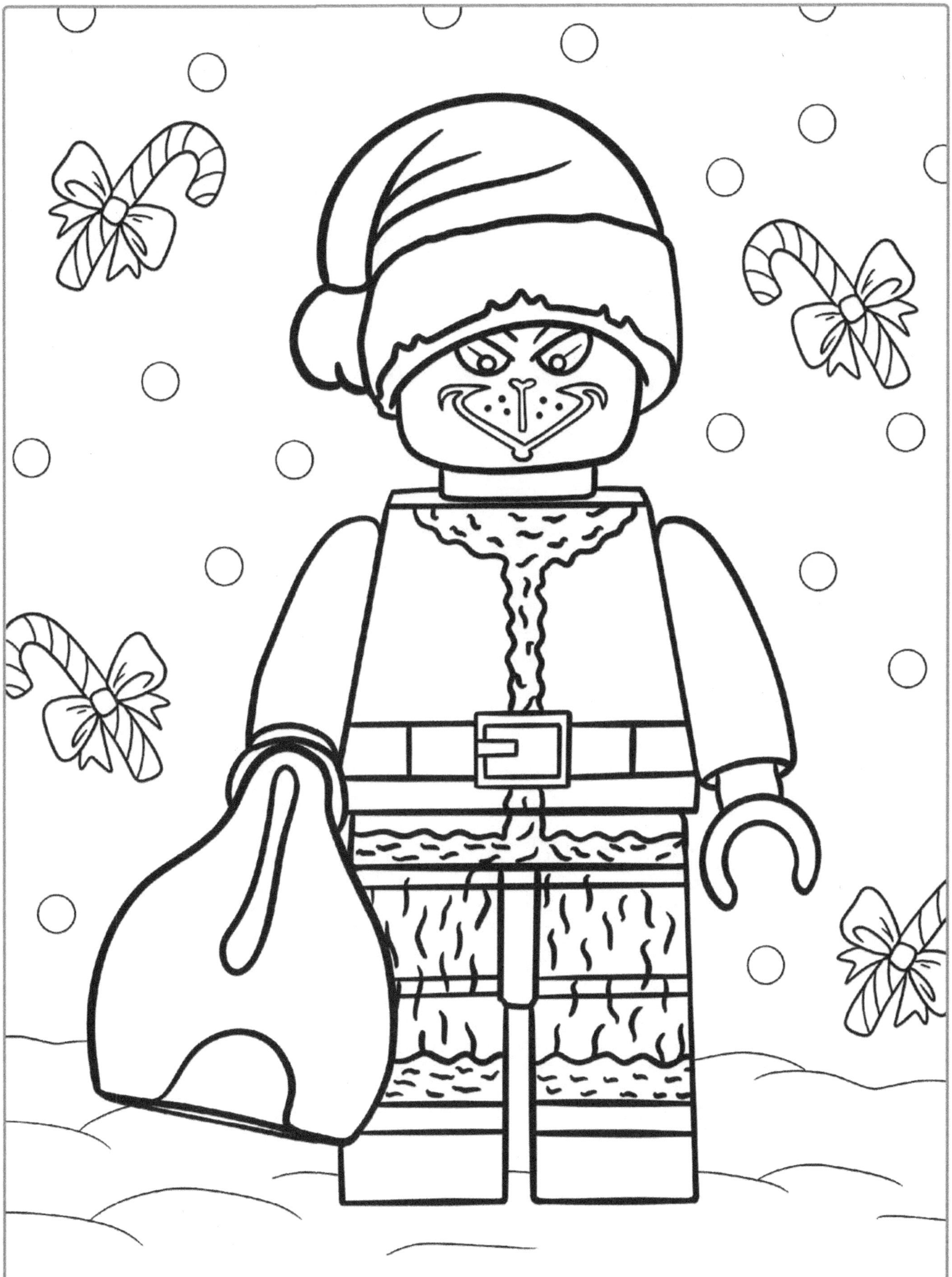

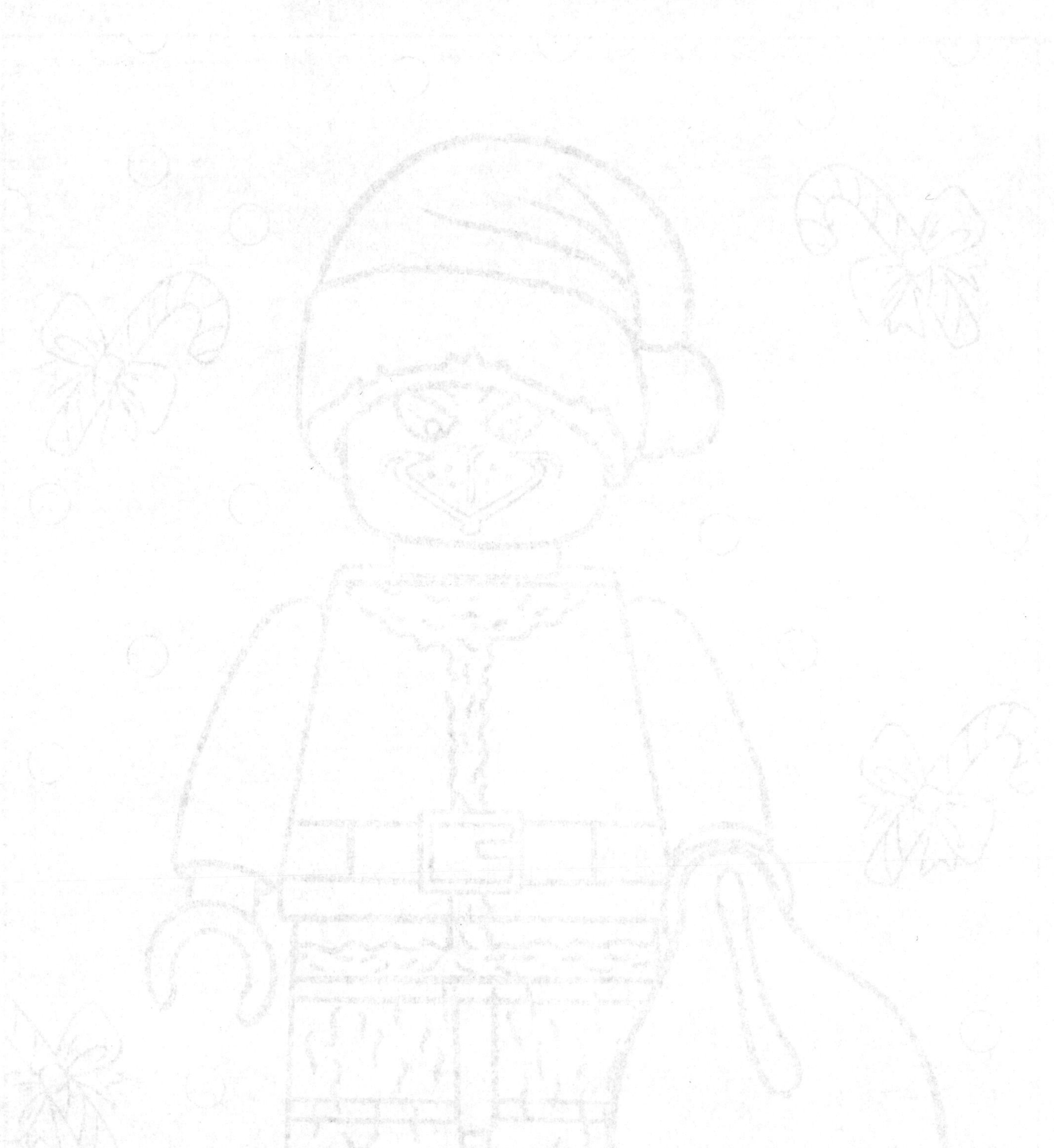

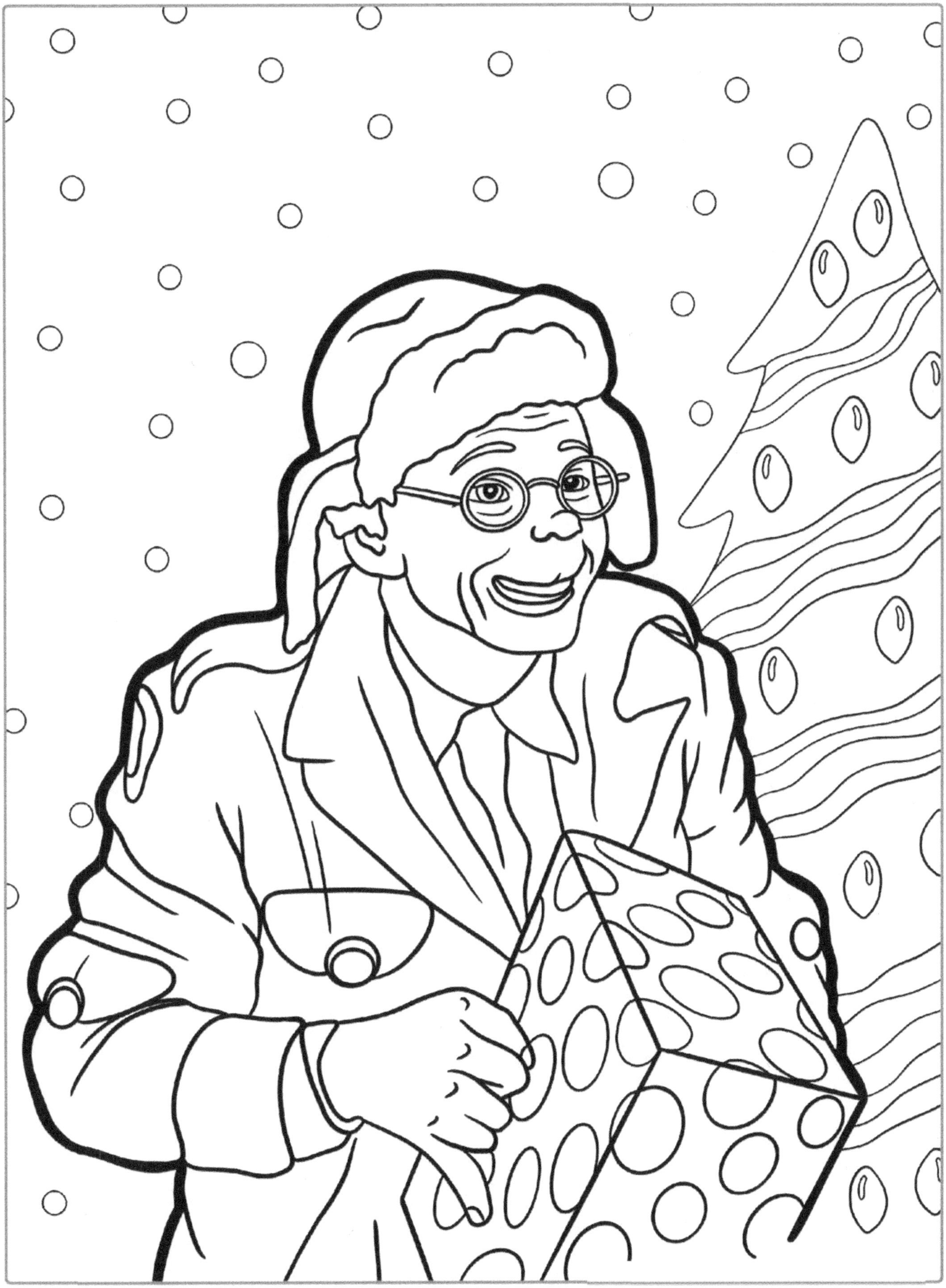

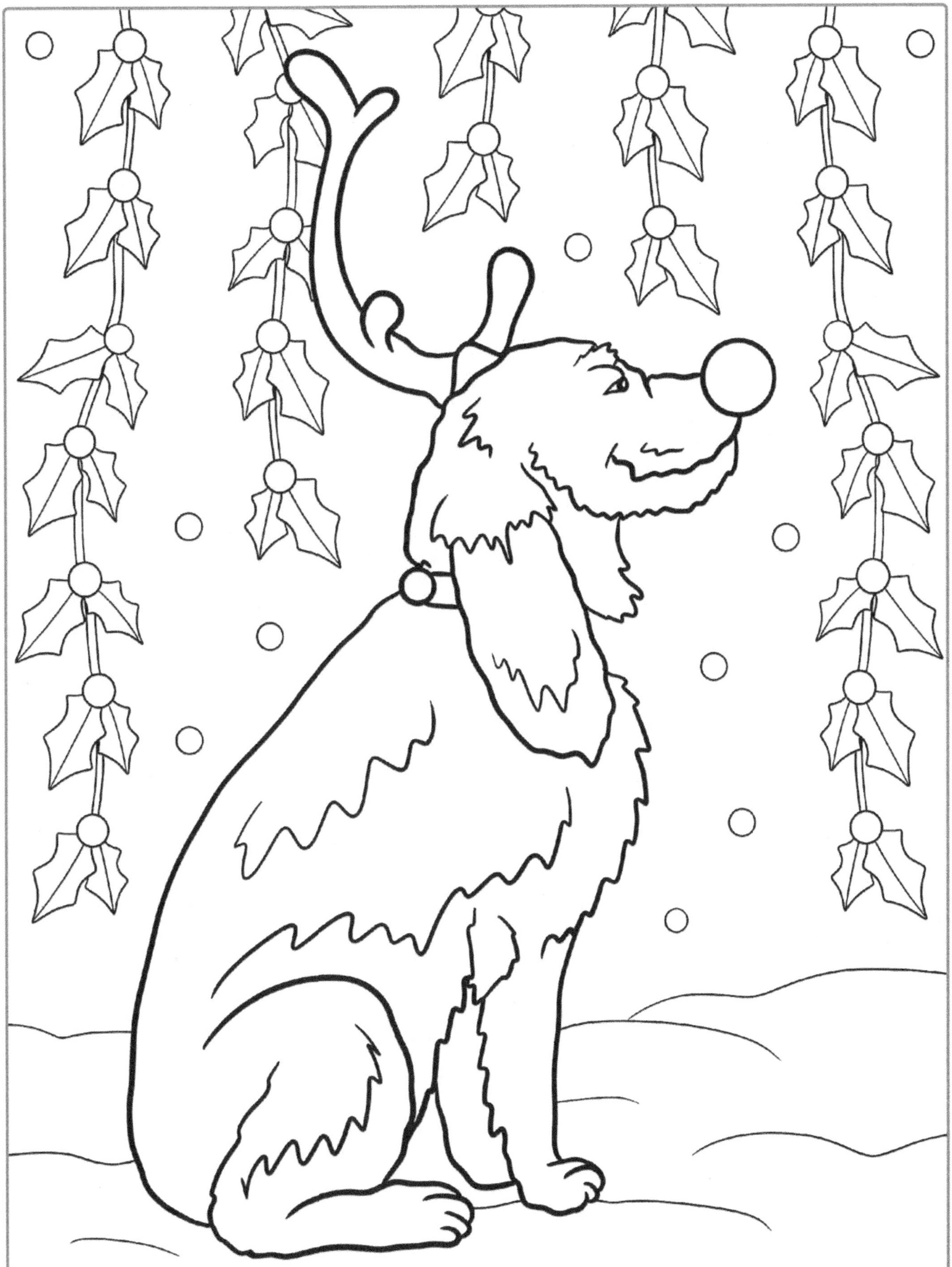

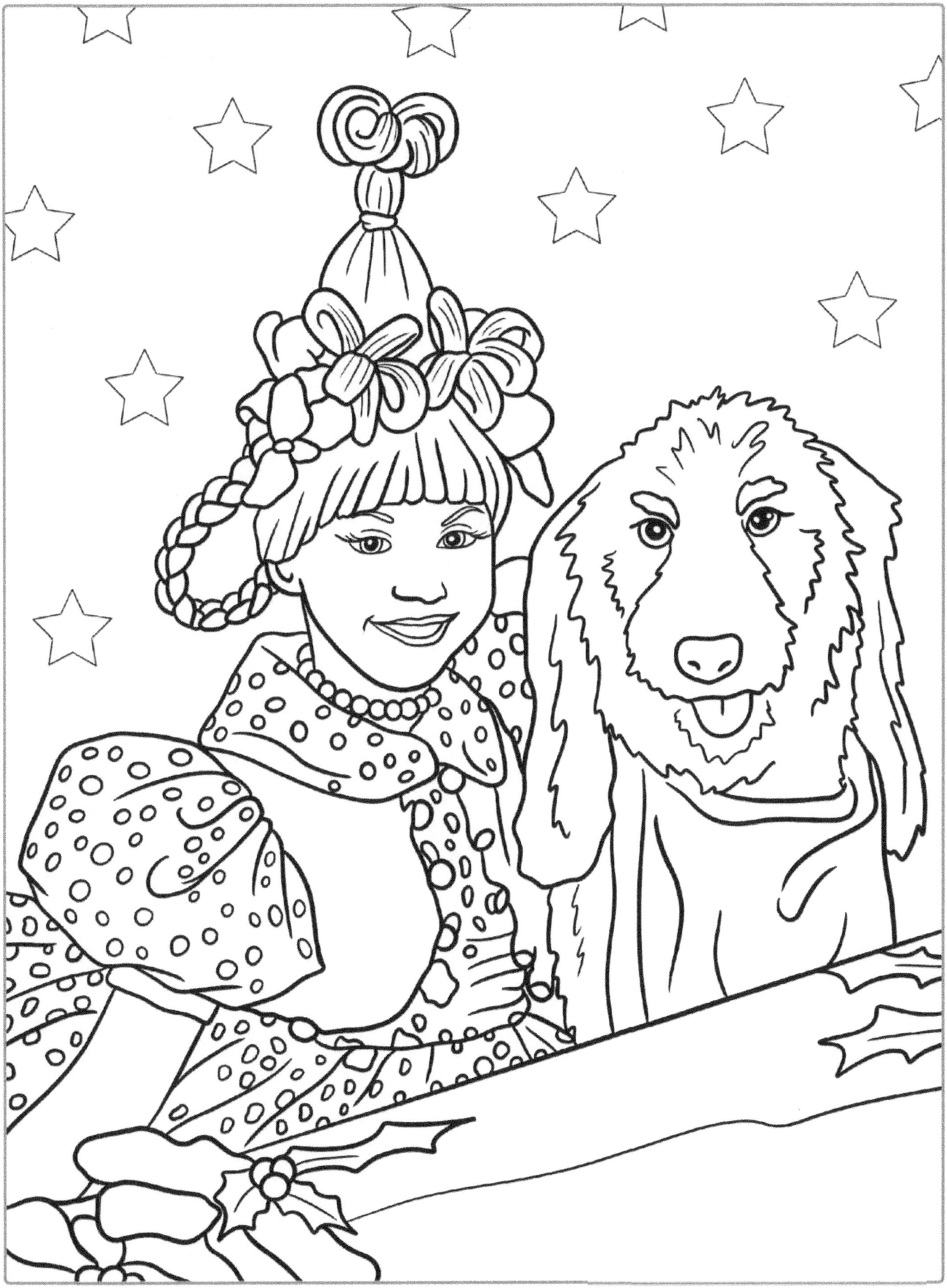

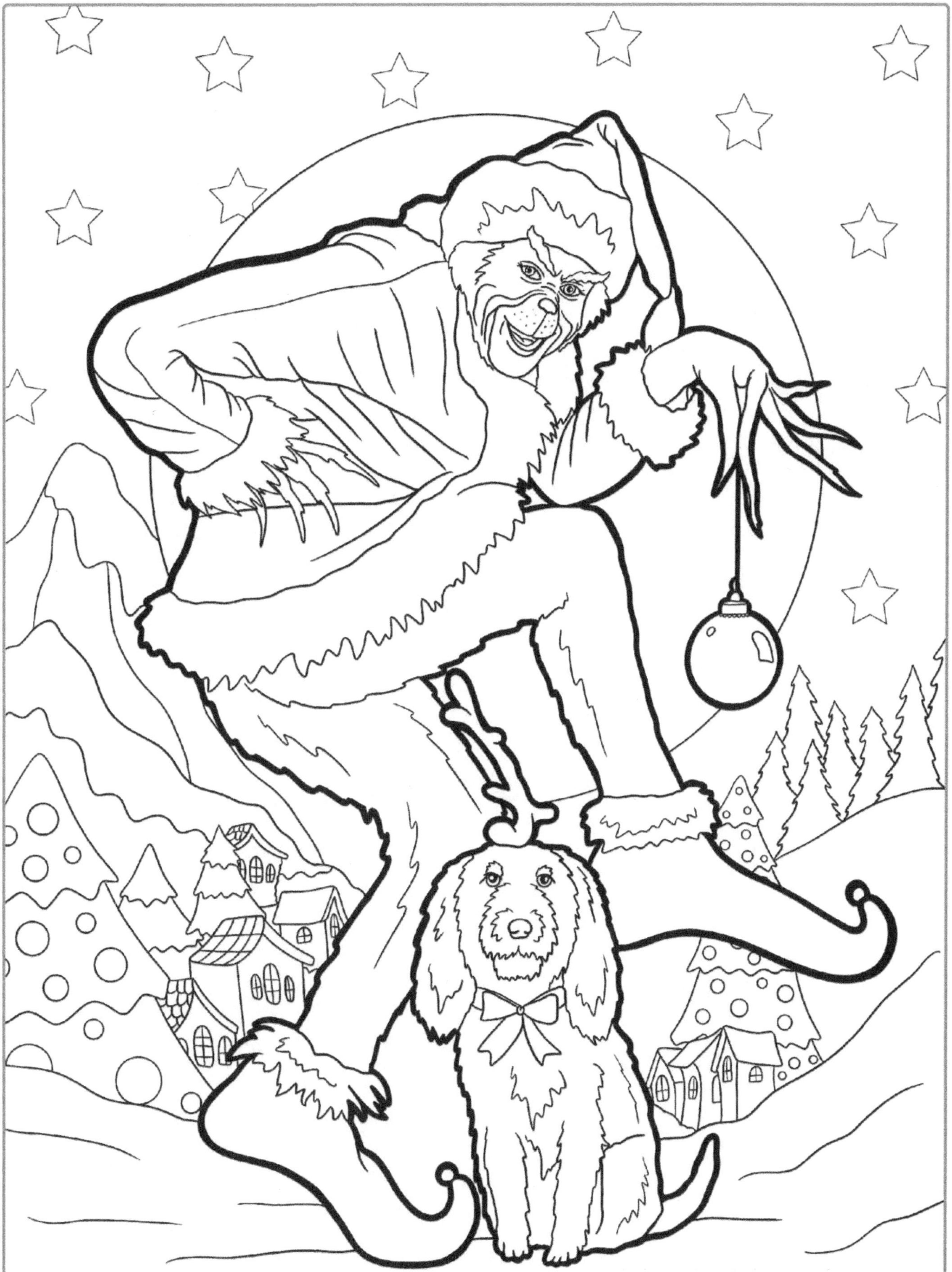

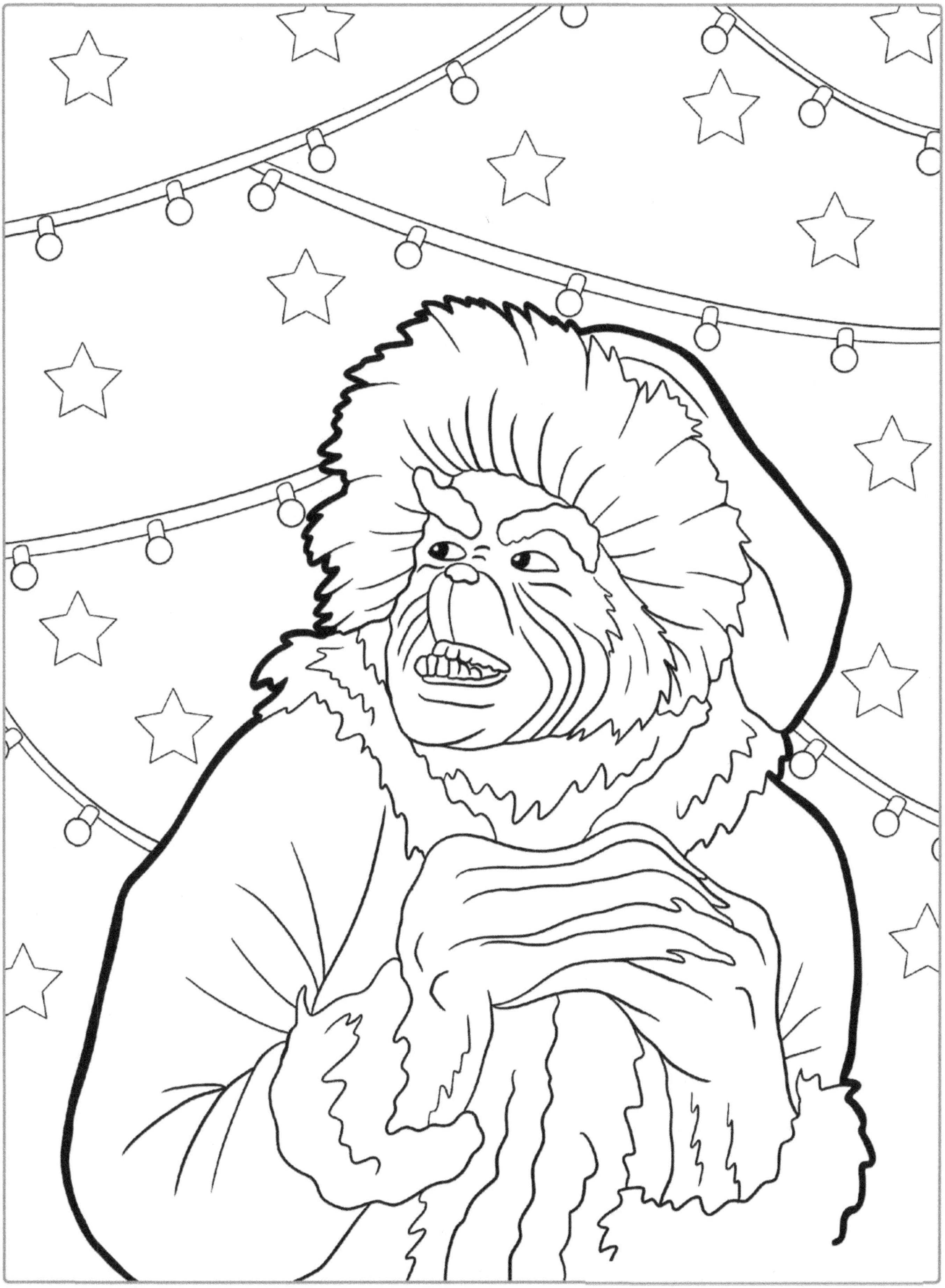

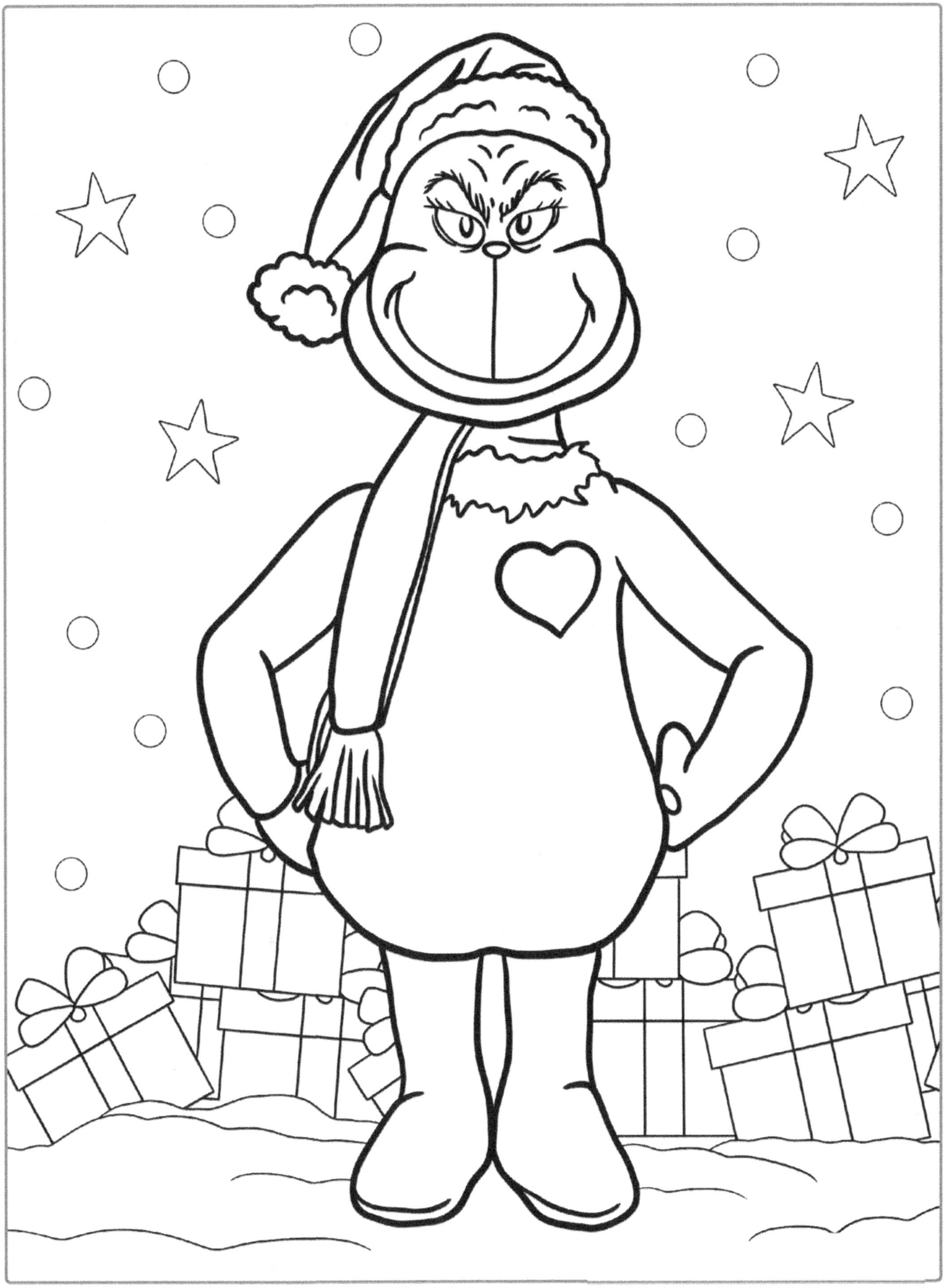

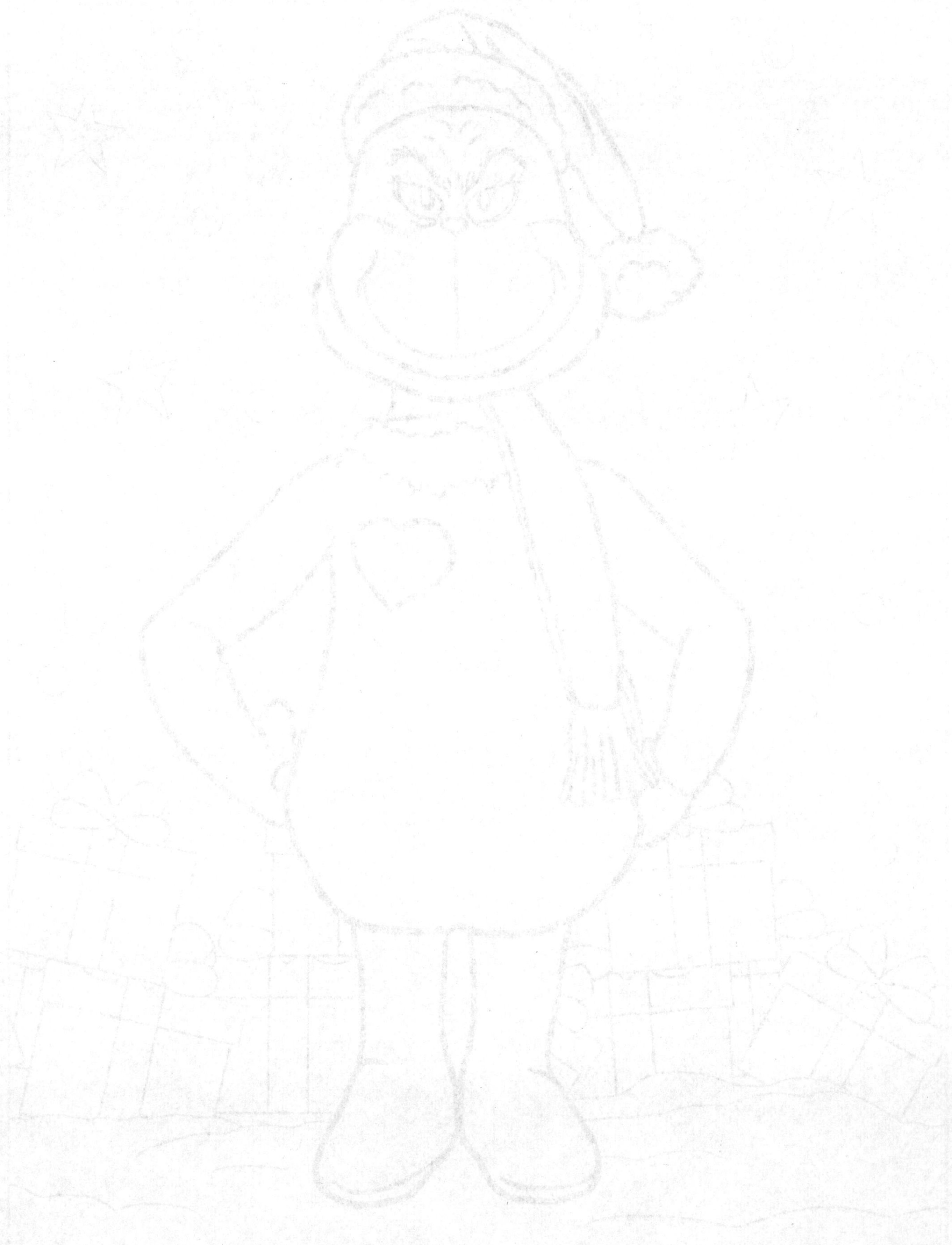

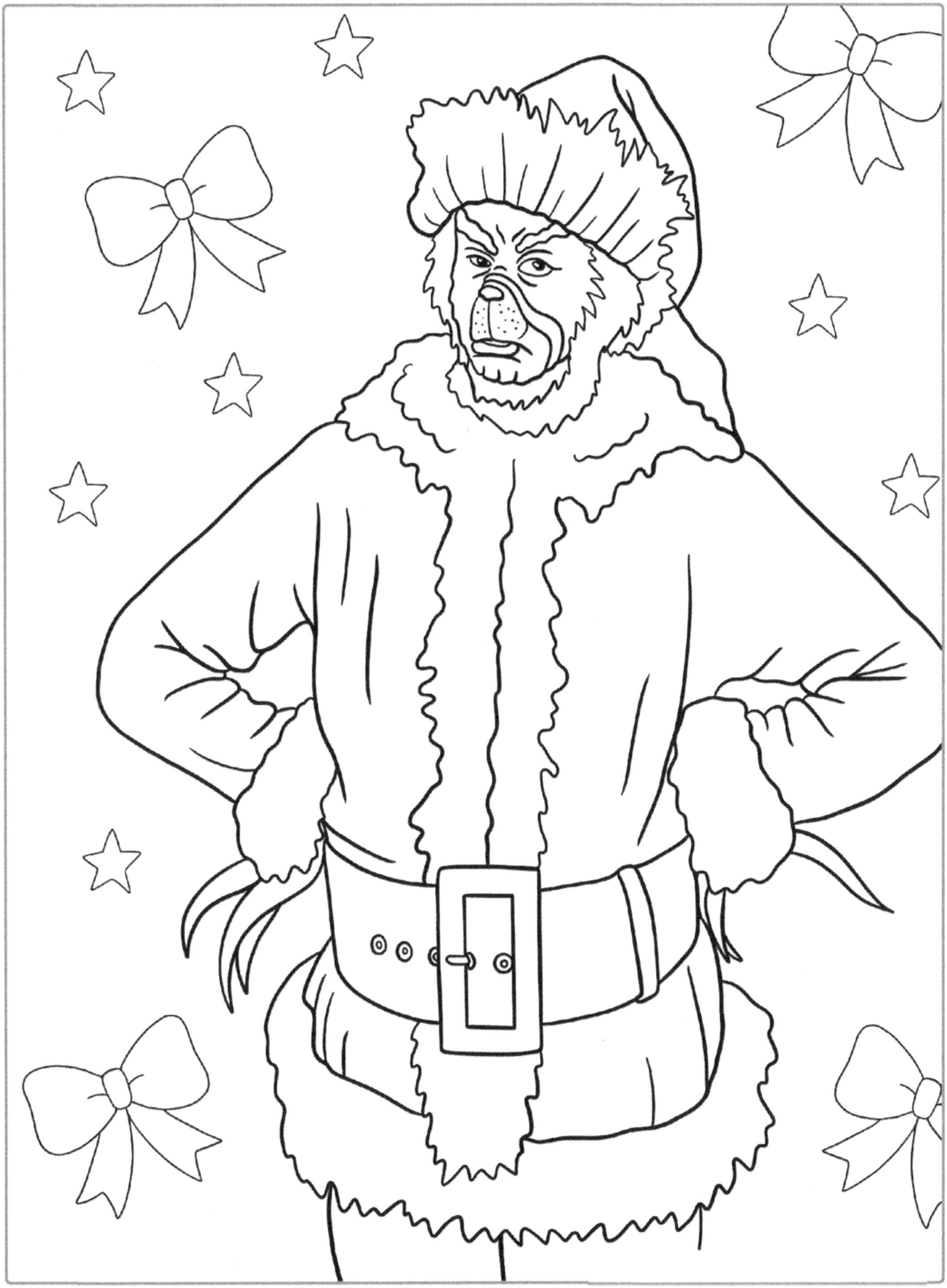

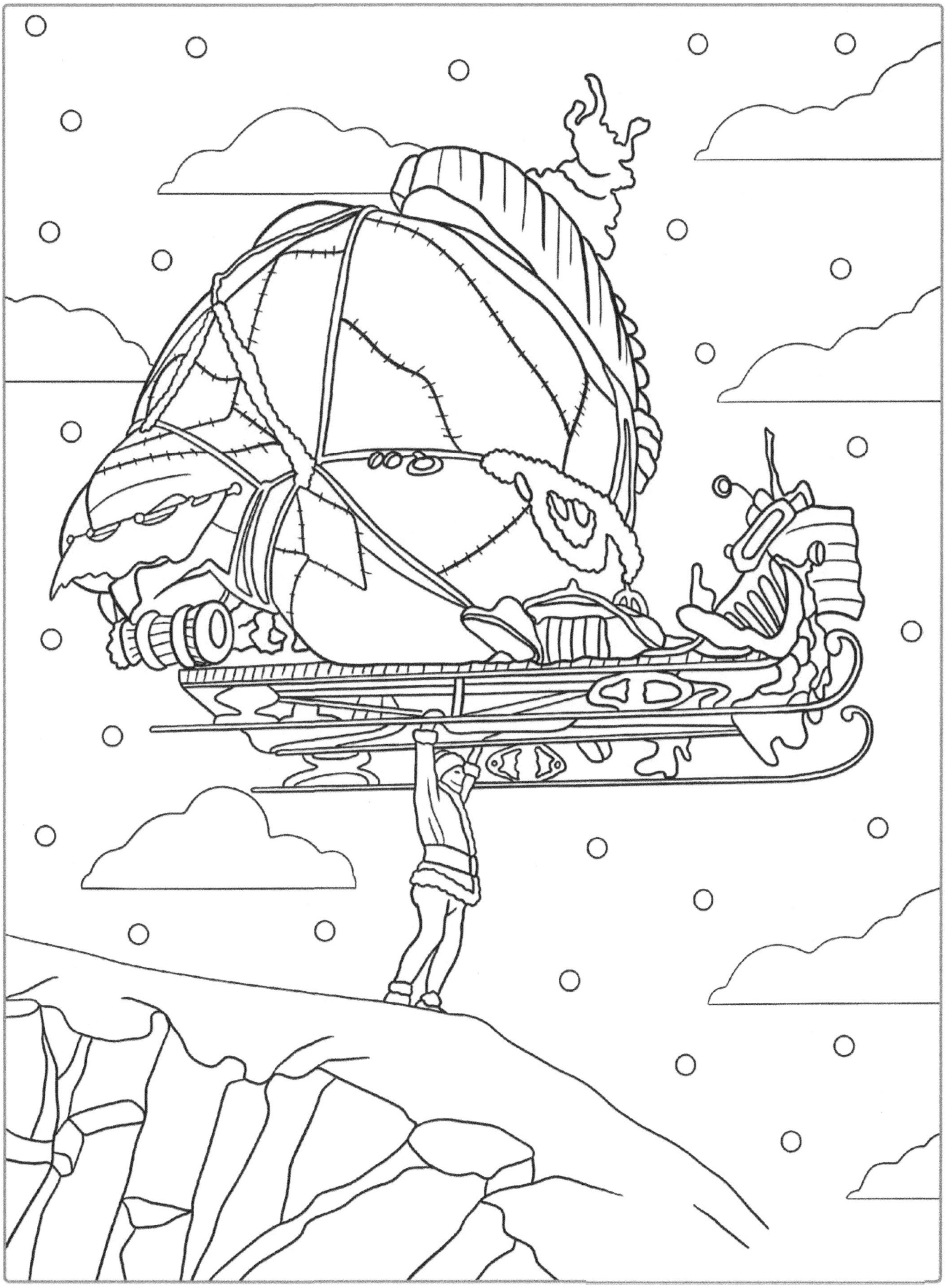

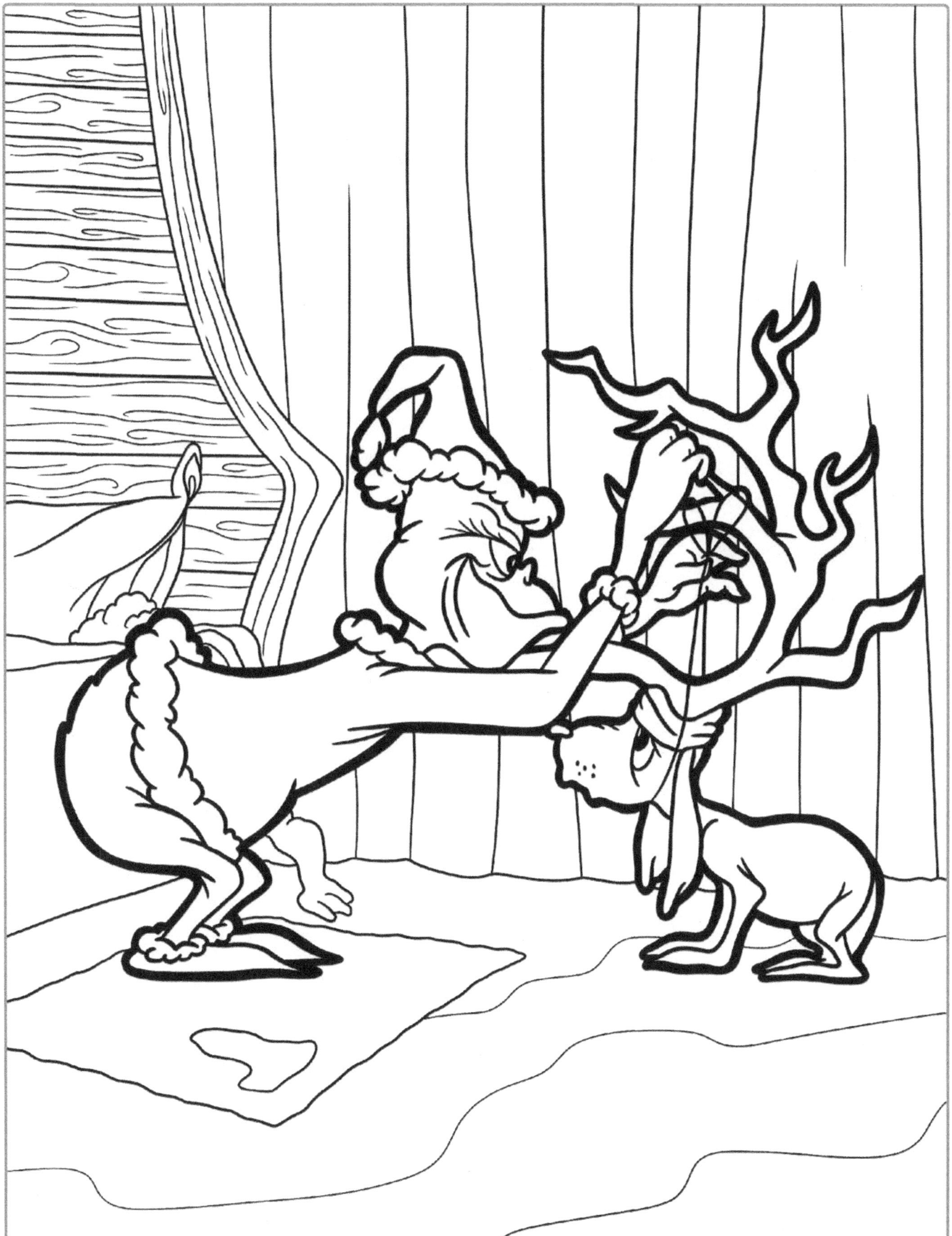

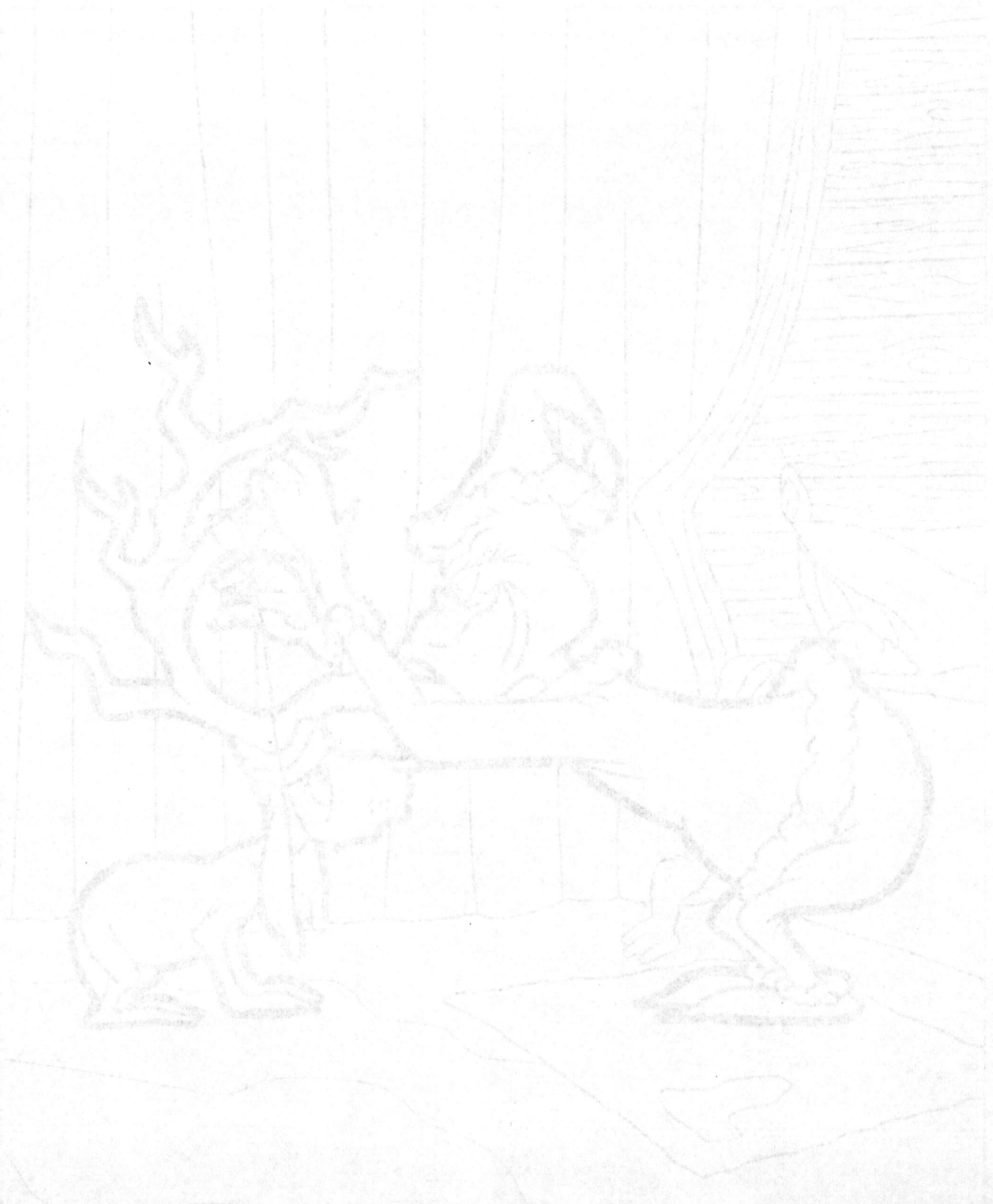

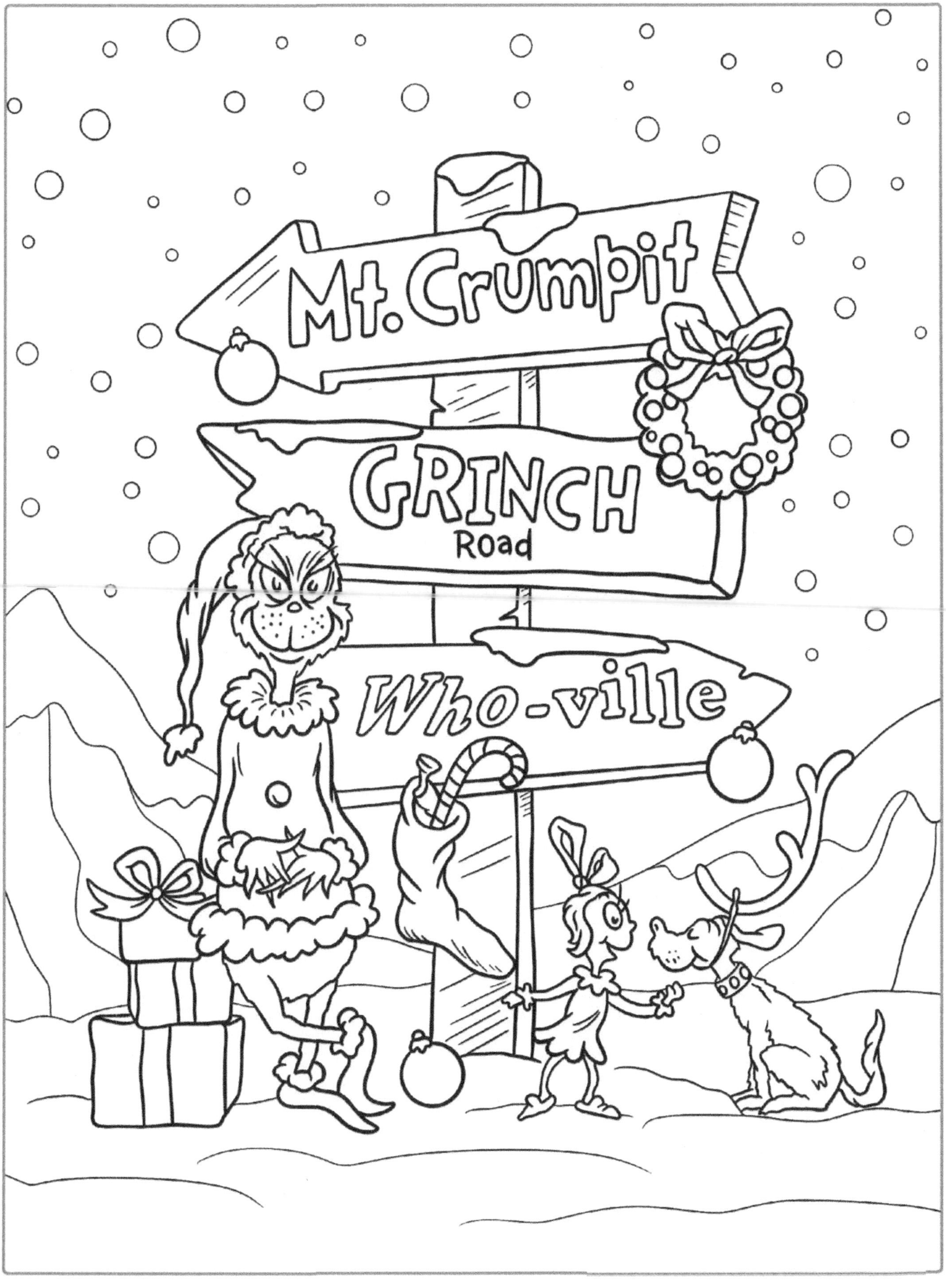
Mt. Crumpit
GRINCH
Road
Who-ville

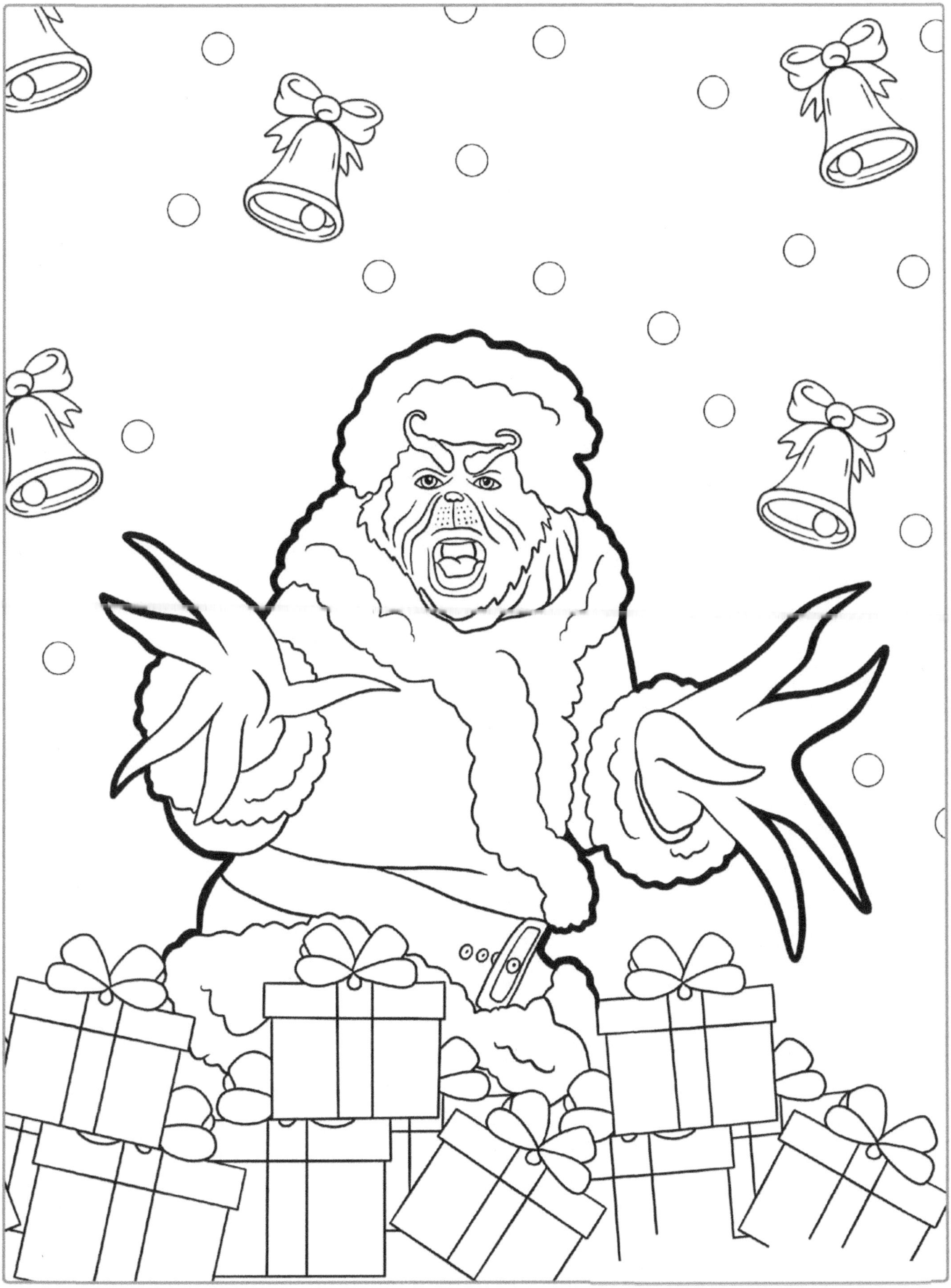

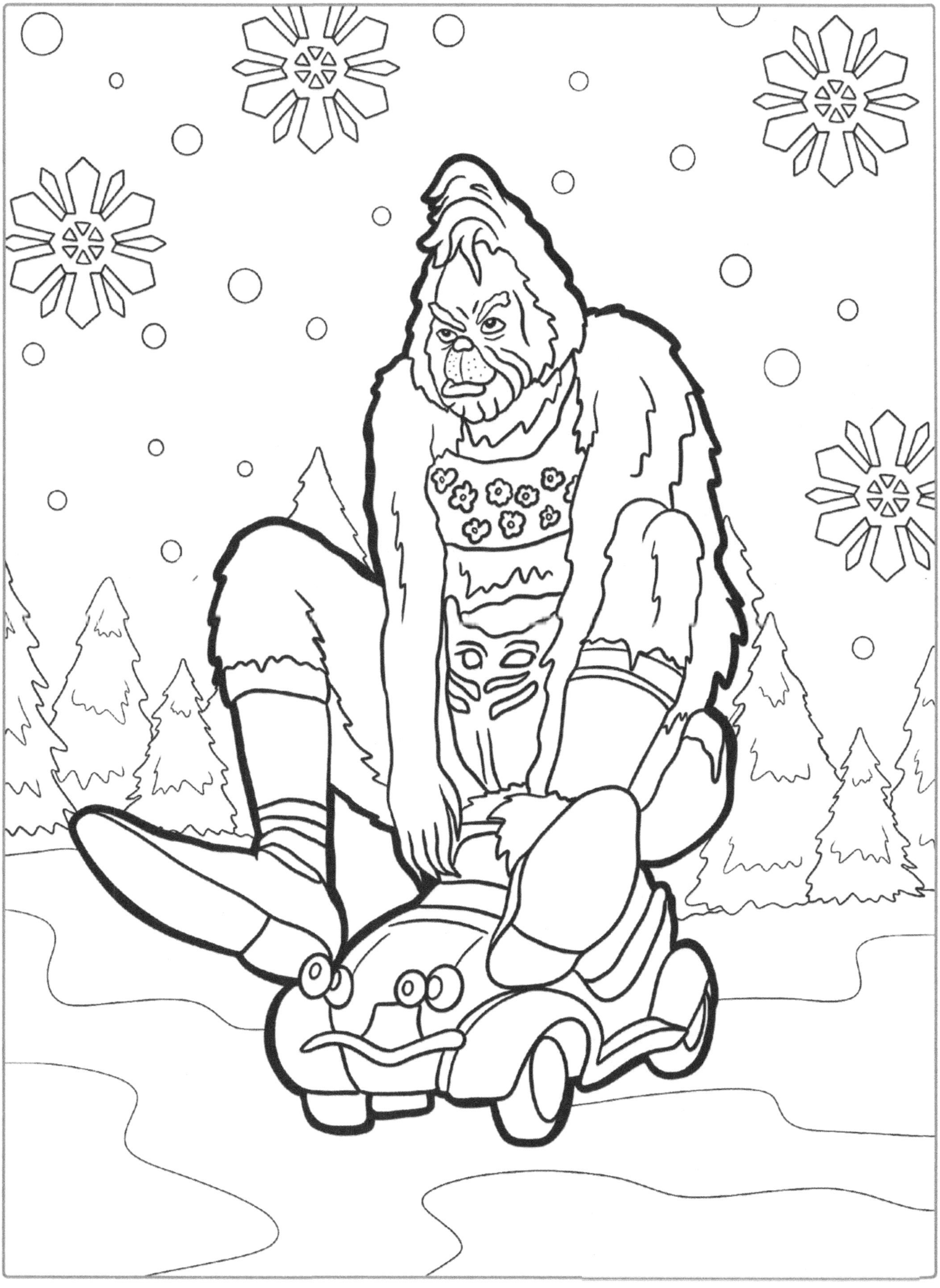

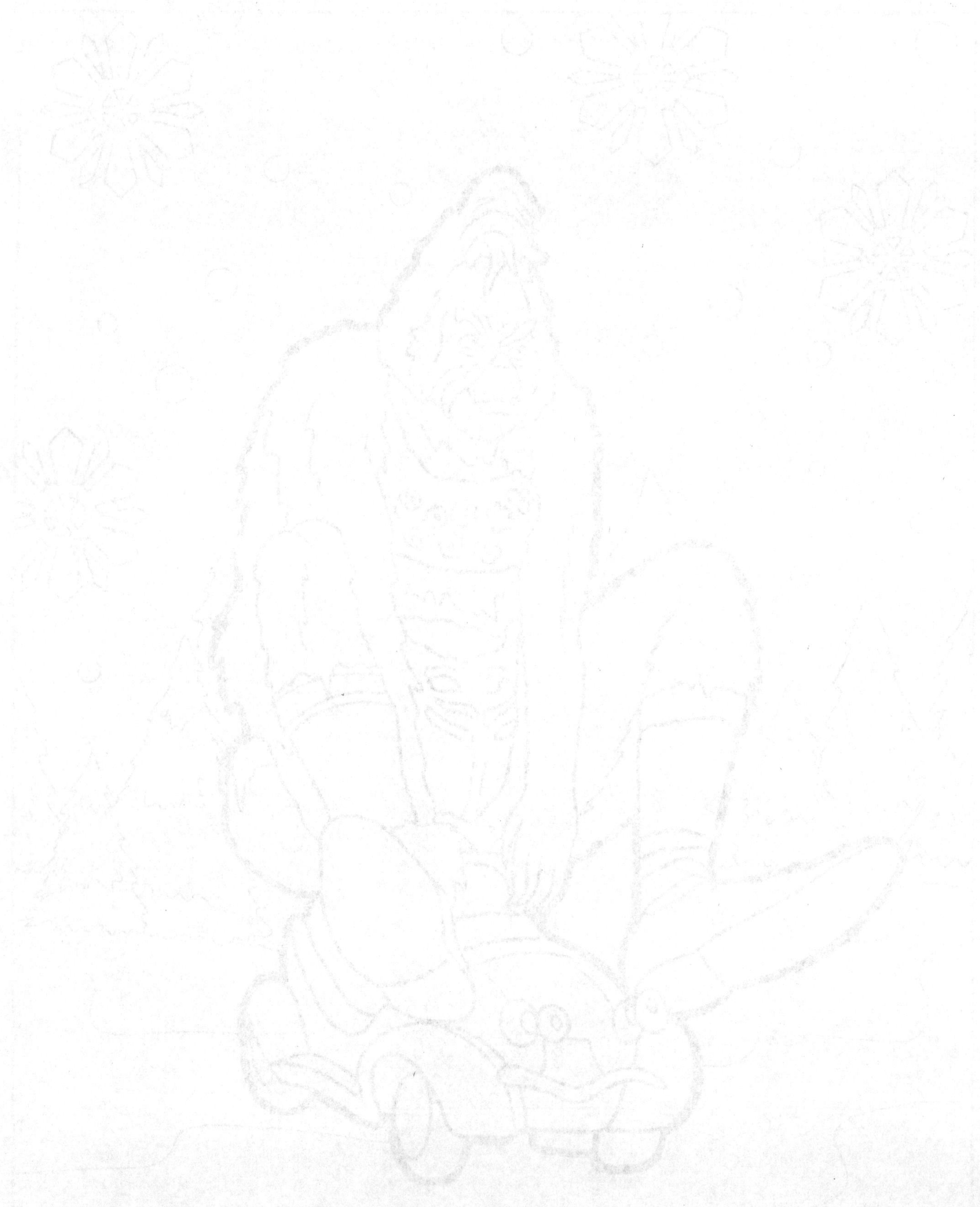

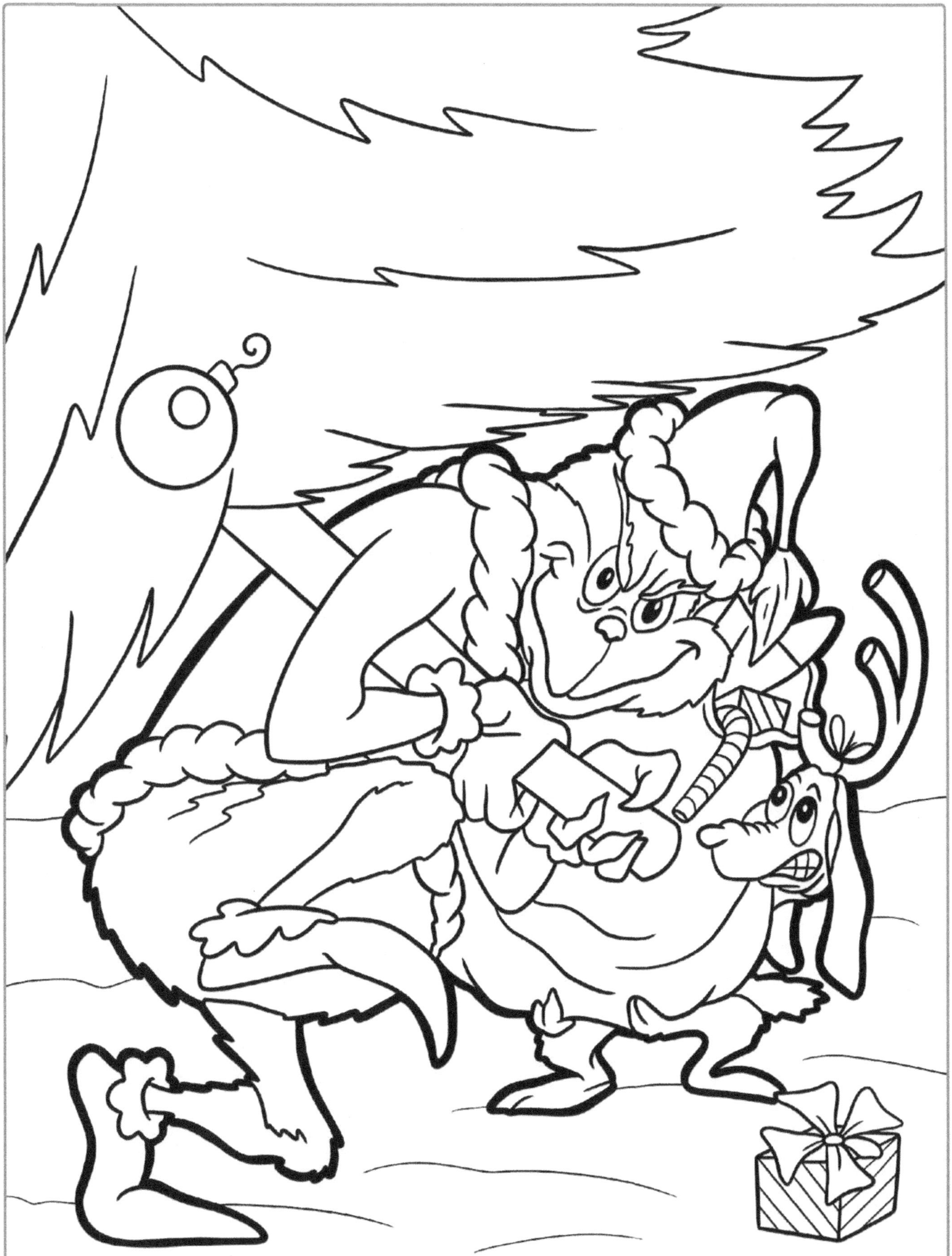

Made in the USA
Las Vegas, NV
11 December 2024

13799593R00044